W9-AHH-559

# Donna Kooler's

# CROSS-STITCH
# FLOWERS

*Donna Kooler's*

# Cross-Stitch Flowers

# A LARK/CHAPELLE BOOK

A Division of Sterling Publishing Co., Inc.

New York

**A Lark/Chapelle Book**

Chapelle, Ltd., Inc.
P.O. Box 9255, Ogden, UT 84409
(801) 621-2777 . (801) 621-2788 Fax
e-mail: chapelle@chapelleltd.com
Web site: www.chapelleltd.com

10 9 8 7 6 5 4 3 2 1

First Edition

Published by Lark Books, A Division of
Sterling Publishing Co., Inc.
387 Park Avenue South, New York, N.Y. 10016

© 2006, Donna Kooler

Distributed in Canada by Sterling Publishing,
c/o Canadian Manda Group, 165 Dufferin Street
Toronto, Ontario, Canada M6K 3H6

Distributed in the United Kingdom by GMC Distribution Services,
Castle Place, 166 High Street, Lewes, East Sussex, England BN7 1XU

Distributed in Australia by Capricorn Link (Australia) Pty Ltd.,
P.O. Box 704, Windsor, NSW 2756 Australia

The written instructions, photographs, designs, patterns, and
projects in this volume are intended for the personal use of the
reader and may be reproduced for that purpose only. Any other use,
especially commercial use, is forbidden under law without written
permission of the copyright holder.

Every effort has been made to ensure that all the information in this
book is accurate. However, due to differing conditions, tools, and
individual skills, the publisher cannot be responsible for any injuries,
losses, and other damages that may result from the use of the
information in this book.

Manufactured in China

All rights reserved

ISBN 13: 978-1-57990-984-0
ISBN 10: 1-57990-984-1

For information about custom editions, special sales, premium and
corporate purchases, please contact Sterling Special Sales
Department at 800-805-5489 or specialsales@sterlingpub.com.

# TABLE of CONTENTS

# INTRODUCTION

Flowers, flowers, flowers—everywhere I look there are beautiful blossoms to be stitched. What a joy it was to produce this book since flowers have been the inspiration for so many of our designs over the years. Turn the pages and virtually walk through our garden of color, size, and variety that even a florist would surely envy, all designed by our outstanding group of award-winning designers: Linda Gillum, Sandy Orton, Barbara Baatz Hillman, Nancy Rossi, and Jorja Hernandez.

As fresh as dewdrops on a spring morning, the projects are sure to please. From magnificent roses and lilies to colorful mixed bouquets, there is something here for everyone. Enjoy.

# GENERAL INSTRUCTIONS

## CROSS-STITCH ITEMS TO KNOW

### FABRIC FOR CROSS-STITCH

Counted cross-stitch is worked on even-weave fabrics. These fabrics are manufactured specifically for counted-thread embroidery, and are woven with the same number of vertical as horizontal threads per inch.

Because the number of threads in the fabric is equal in each direction, each stitch will be the same size. The number of threads per inch in even-weave fabrics determines the size of a finished design.

### NUMBER OF FLOSS STRANDS

The number of floss strands used per stitch varies, depending on the fabric used. Generally, the rule to follow for cross-stitching is three strands of floss on Aida 11, two strands on Aida 14, one or two strands on Aida 18 (depending on desired thickness of stitches), and one strand on Hardanger 22.

For backstitching, use one strand on all fabrics. When completing a French Knot (FK), use one strand and one wrap on all fabrics, unless otherwise directed.

### FINISHED DESIGN SIZE

To determine the size of the finished design, divide the stitch count by the number of threads per inch of fabric. When a design is stitched over two threads, divide the stitch count by half the threads per inch. For example, if a design with a stitch count of 120 width and 250 height was stitched on a 28-count linen (over two threads, making it 14 count), the finished size would be $8\frac{5}{8}$" x $17\frac{7}{8}$".

$120 \div 14" = 8\frac{5}{8}"$ (width)

$250 \div 14" = 17\frac{7}{8}"$ (height)

Finished size = $8\frac{5}{8}"$ x $17\frac{7}{8}"$

### PREPARING FABRIC

Cut fabric at least 3" larger on all sides than the finished design size to ensure enough space for desired assembly. To prevent fraying, whip-stitch or machine-zigzag along the raw edges or apply liquid fray preventive.

### NEEDLES FOR CROSS-STITCH

Blunt needles should slip easily through the fabric holes without piercing fabric threads. For fabric with 11 or fewer threads per inch, use a tapestry needle #24; for 14 threads per inch, use a tapestry needle #24, #26, or #28; for 18 or more threads per inch, use a tapestry needle #26 or #28. Avoid leaving the needle in the design area of the fabric. It may leave rust or a permanent impression on the fabric.

## Floss

All numbers and color names on the codes represent the DMC brand of floss. Use 18" lengths of floss. For best coverage, separate the strands and dampen with a wet sponge, then put together the number of strands required for the fabric used.

## Centering Design on Fabric

Fold the fabric in half horizontally, then vertically. Place a pin in the intersection to mark the center. Locate the center of the design on the graph. To help in centering the designs, arrows are provided at the center top and center side. Begin stitching all designs at the center point of the graph and fabric.

## Securing Floss

Insert needle up from the underside of the fabric at starting point. Hold 1" of thread behind the fabric and stitch over it, securing with the first few stitches. To finish thread, run under four or more stitches on the back of the design. Avoid knotting floss, unless working on clothing.

Another method of securing floss is the waste knot. Knot floss and insert needle down from the top left side of the fabric about 1" from design area. Work area. Cut off the knot and secure thread under worked stitches.

## Carrying Floss

To carry floss, run floss under the previously worked stitches on the back. Do not carry thread across any fabric that is not or will not be stitched. Loose threads, especially dark ones, will show through the fabric.

## Cleaning Finished Design

When stitching is finished, soak the fabric in cold water with a mild soap for five to ten minutes. Rinse well and roll in a towel to remove excess water. Do not wring. Place the piece face down on a dry towel and iron on a warm setting until the fabric is dry.

## Stitching Techniques

### Backstitch (BS)

1. Insert the needle up between woven threads at A.

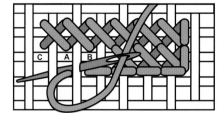

2. Go down at B, one opening to the right.

3. Come up at C.

4. Go down at A, one opening to the right.

### Baste Stitch

1. Insert needle up through fabric at A, using one strand of sewing thread.

2. Go down at B, creating a line of long straight stitches.

3. Come up at C, leaving an unstitched area between each stitch. Repeat.

### Bead Attachment (BD)

Beads should sit facing the same direction as the top cross-stitch.

1. Make first half of cross-stitch.

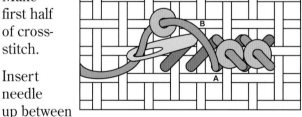

2. Insert needle up between woven threads at A.

3. Thread on bead before going down at B, the opening diagonally across from A.

4. To strengthen stitch, come up again at A and either go through bead again or if the floss is doubled, split floss to lay around bead and go down at B again.

## CROSS-STITCH (XS)

Stitches are done in a row or, if necessary, one at a time in an area.

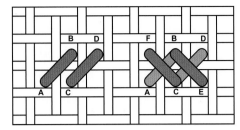

1. Insert needle up between woven threads at A.

2. Go down at B, one opening diagonally across from A.

3. Come up at C and go down at D, etc.

4. To complete the top stitches creating an "X", come up at E and go down at B, come up at C and go down at F, etc. All top stitches should lie in the same direction.

## FRENCH KNOT (FK)

1. Insert the needle up between the woven threads at A, using one strand of the embroidery floss.

2. Loosely wrap floss once around needle.

3. Go down at B, one opening across from A. Pull floss taut as needle is pushed down through fabric.

4. Carry floss across back of work between knots.

## QUARTER STITCH (QS)

Quarter stitches are ¼ of a regular cross-stitch.

1. Insert needle up between woven threads at A.

2. Split the fabric thread to go down at B.

## RUNNING STITCH

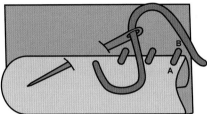

1. Bring needle up through the fabric. Insert needle down through fabric, creating a straight stitch. Repeat, leaving an unstitched area between each stitch.

## SLIPSTITCH

1. Insert needle up between fold at A.

2. Go down at B and slide needle between fold for ⅛" to ¼".

3. Bring needle out through both folds at same level as A, but over a small distance as shown in diagram.

4. Draw up thread gently to secure a closed joint, too hard will pucker fabric.

5. Repeat stitch across entire opening, keeping stitches between ⅛" and ¼" apart.

## STRAIGHT STITCH (SS)

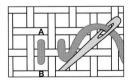

1. Bring needle up between the woven threads at A.

2. Go down at B. *Note: This stitch can be worked in any direction over any threads.*

## ZIGZAG STITCH

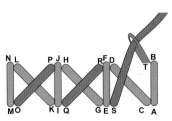

1. Insert needle up through fabric at A, using three strands of thread.

2. Go down at B.

3. Come up at C. Go down at D, diagonally.

4. Repeat working right to left. Repeat length, working left to right.

# COASTERS

## MATERIALS & SUPPLIES
(for one coaster)

- Acrylic coaster (or wooden box as desired)
- Desired cross-stitch fabric
- Fabric hoop
- Fabric scissors
- Iron/ironing board

## INSTRUCTIONS
(for one coaster)

1. With fabric in hoop, stitch desired design,

2. Remove cross-stitched piece from fabric hoop. Press, right side down.

3. Insert into coaster, following manufacturer's instructions.

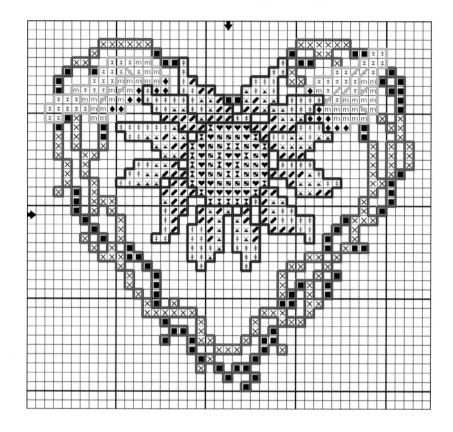

## STITCHING INFORMATION

Fabric: Aida 14, white

Stitch Count: 41w x 38h

Size: 14 count, 2⅞" x 2⅝"

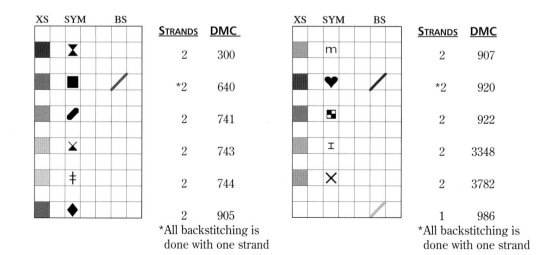

| XS | SYM | BS | STRANDS | DMC |
|----|-----|----|---------|-----|
| | ✕ | | 2 | 300 |
| | ■ | ╱ | *2 | 640 |
| | ◗ | | 2 | 741 |
| | ✕ | | 2 | 743 |
| | ‡ | | 2 | 744 |
| | ◆ | | 2 | 905 |

*All backstitching is done with one strand

| XS | SYM | BS | STRANDS | DMC |
|----|-----|----|---------|-----|
| | m | | 2 | 907 |
| | ♥ | ╱ | *2 | 920 |
| | ◨ | | 2 | 922 |
| | I | | 2 | 3348 |
| | ✕ | | 2 | 3782 |
| | | ╱ | 1 | 986 |

*All backstitching is done with one strand

# SCALLOPED COASTER

## STITCHING INFORMATION

Fabric: Aida 14, white

Stitch Count: 39w x 40h

Size: 14 count, 2¾" square

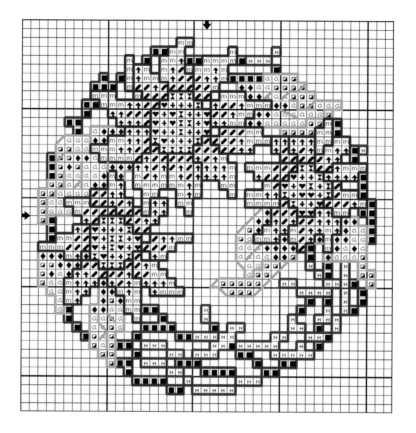

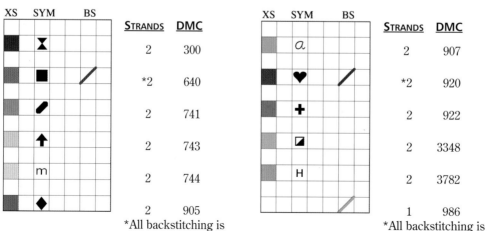

| XS | SYM | BS | STRANDS | DMC |
|---|---|---|---|---|
| | ✕ | | 2 | 300 |
| | ■ | ╱ | *2 | 640 |
| | ◖ | | 2 | 741 |
| | ↑ | | 2 | 743 |
| | m | | 2 | 744 |
| | ◆ | | 2 | 905 |

*All backstitching is
done with one strand

| XS | SYM | BS | STRANDS | DMC |
|---|---|---|---|---|
| | a | | 2 | 907 |
| | ♥ | ╱ | *2 | 920 |
| | ✚ | | 2 | 922 |
| | ◣ | | 2 | 3348 |
| | H | | 2 | 3782 |
| | | ╱ | 1 | 986 |

*All backstitching is
done with one strand

# Star Coaster

## Stitching Information

Fabric: Aida 14, white

Stitch count: 46w x 42h

Size: 14 count, 3¼" x 3"

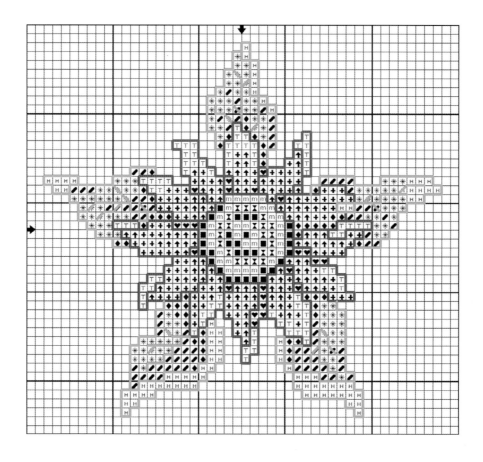

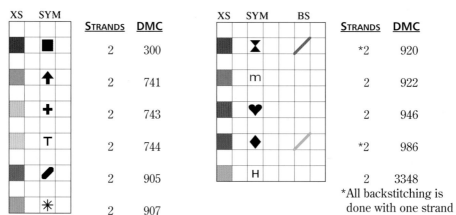

| XS | SYM | STRANDS | DMC |
|---|---|---|---|
| ■ (dark) | ■ | 2 | 300 |
| ■ | ↑ | 2 | 741 |
| ■ | ✚ | 2 | 743 |
| ■ | T | 2 | 744 |
| ■ | ◤ | 2 | 905 |
| ■ | ✱ | 2 | 907 |

*All backstitching is done with one strand

| XS | SYM | BS | STRANDS | DMC |
|---|---|---|---|---|
| ■ | ✖ | / | *2 | 920 |
| ■ | m | | 2 | 922 |
| ■ | ♥ | | 2 | 946 |
| ■ | ◆ | / | *2 | 986 |
| ■ | H | | 2 | 3348 |

*All backstitching is done with one strand

# SHRUB ROSE COASTER

## STITCHING INFORMATION

Fabric: Aida 14, white

Stitch Count: 38w x 36h

Size: 14 count, 2⅝" x 2½"

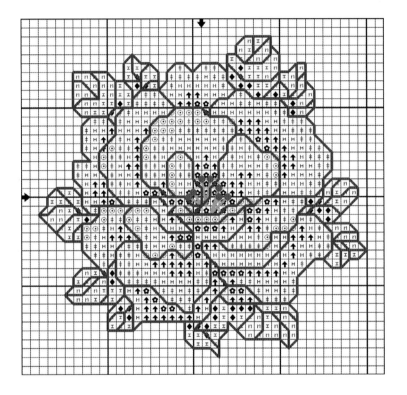

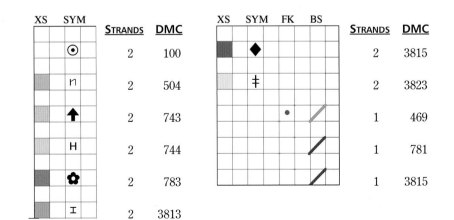

| XS | SYM | STRANDS | DMC |
|----|-----|---------|-----|
| | ⊙ | 2 | 100 |
| | n | 2 | 504 |
| | ↑ | 2 | 743 |
| | H | 2 | 744 |
| | ✿ | 2 | 783 |
| | I | 2 | 3813 |

| XS | SYM | FK | BS | STRANDS | DMC |
|----|-----|----|----|---------|-----|
| | ◆ | | | 2 | 3815 |
| | ‡ | | | 2 | 3823 |
| | | • | / | 1 | 469 |
| | | | / | 1 | 781 |
| | | | / | 1 | 3815 |

# PINK CABBAGE COASTER

## STITCHING INFORMATION

Fabric: Aida 14, white

Stitch Count: 40w x 40h

Size: 14 count, 2¾" square

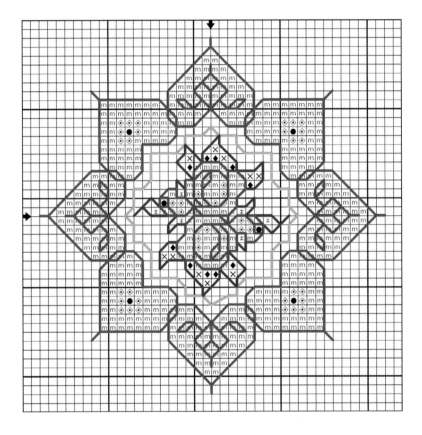

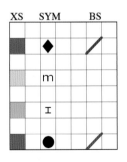
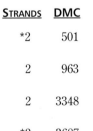

| XS | SYM | BS | STRANDS | DMC |
|---|---|---|---|---|
| | ◆ | / | *2 | 501 |
| | m | | 2 | 963 |
| | I | | 2 | 3348 |
| | ● | / | *2 | 3687 |

*All backstitching is
done with one strand

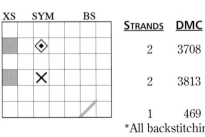

| XS | SYM | BS | STRANDS | DMC |
|---|---|---|---|---|
| | ◈ | | 2 | 3708 |
| | ✕ | | 2 | 3813 |
| | | / | 1 | 469 |

*All backstitching is
done with one strand

## STITCHING INFORMATION

Fabric: Aida 14, white

Stitch Count: 42w x 42h

Size: 14 count, 3" square

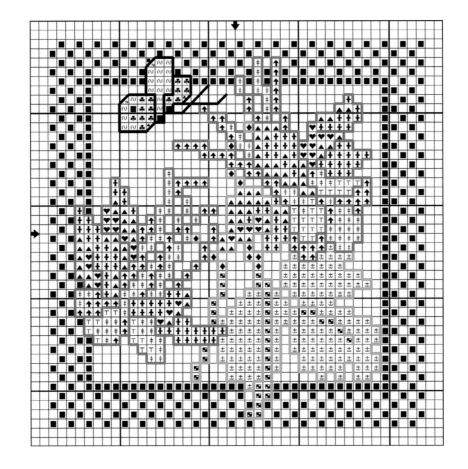

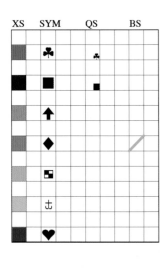

| XS | SYM | QS | BS | STRANDS | DMC |
|----|-----|-----|-----|---------|-----|
| | ♣ | ♣ | | *2 | 208 |
| | ■ | ■ | | 2 | 310 |
| | ↑ | | | 2 | 436 |
| | ◆ | | / | *2 | 562 |
| | ▣ | | | 2 | 563 |
| | ⚓ | | | 2 | 564 |
| | ♥ | | | 2 | 666 |

*All backstitching is
done with one strand

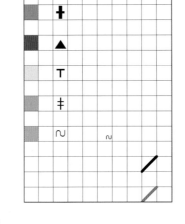

| XS | SYM | QS | BS | STRANDS | DMC |
|----|-----|-----|-----|---------|-----|
| | ✝ | | | 2 | 741 |
| | ▲ | | | 2 | 947 |
| | T | | | 2 | 3823 |
| | ‡ | | | 2 | 3827 |
| | ~ | ~ | | 2 | 210 plus 1 strand **032 |
| | | | / | 1 | 413 |
| | | | / | 1 | 3826 |

*All backstitching is
done with one strand
**Kreinik Blending Filament

# BLEEDING HEART COASTER

## STITCHING INFORMATION

Fabric: Aida 14, white

Stitch Count: 42w x 42h

Size: 14 count, 3" square

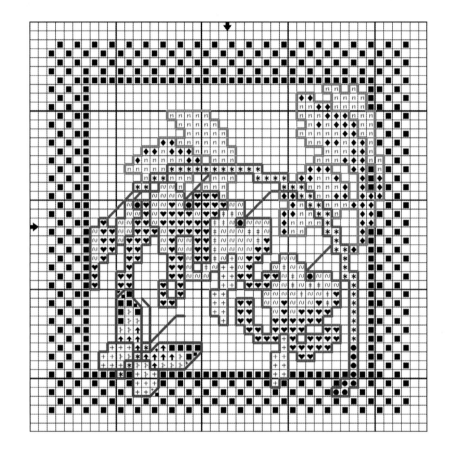

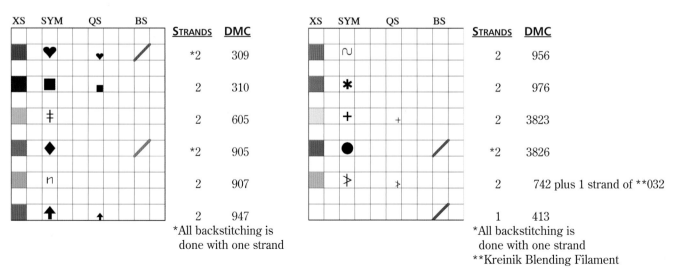

| XS | SYM | QS | BS | | STRANDS | DMC |
|----|-----|----|----|---|---------|-----|
| | ♥ | ♥ | / | | *2 | 309 |
| ■ | ■ | ■ | | | 2 | 310 |
| | ‡ | | | | 2 | 605 |
| | ◆ | | / | | *2 | 905 |
| | n | | | | 2 | 907 |
| | ↑ | ↑ | | | 2 | 947 |

*All backstitching is
  done with one strand

| XS | SYM | QS | BS | | STRANDS | DMC |
|----|-----|----|----|---|---------|-----|
| | ∼ | | | | 2 | 956 |
| | * | | | | 2 | 976 |
| | + | + | | | 2 | 3823 |
| | ● | | / | | *2 | 3826 |
| | ⸸ | ⸸ | | | 2 | 742 plus 1 strand of **032 |
| | | | / | | 1 | 413 |

*All backstitching is
  done with one strand
**Kreinik Blending Filament

22

# CYCLAMEN COASTER

## STITCHING INFORMATION

Fabric: Aida 14, white

Stitch Count: 42w x 42h

Size: 14 count, 3" square

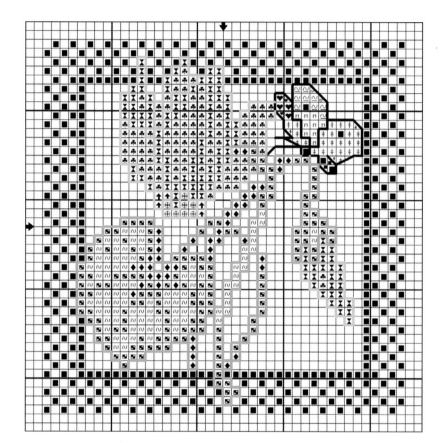

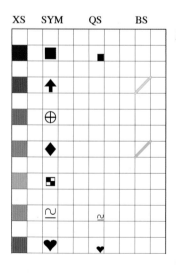

| XS | SYM | QS | BS | STRANDS | DMC |
|----|-----|-----|-----|---------|-----|
| | ■ | ■ | | 2 | 310 |
| | ↑ | | / | *2 | 327 |
| | ⊕ | | | 2 | 553 |
| | ◆ | | / | *2 | 562 |
| | ▣ | | | 2 | 703 |
| | ~ | ~ | | 2 | 741 |
| | ♥ | ♥ | | 2 | 947 |

*All backstitching is
done with one strand

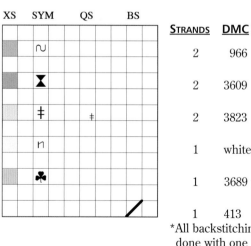

| XS | SYM | QS | BS | STRANDS | DMC |
|----|-----|-----|-----|---------|-----|
| | ~ | | | 2 | 966 |
| | ✕ | | | 2 | 3609 |
| | ‡ | ‡ | | 2 | 3823 |
| | n | | | 1 | white plus 1 strand **032 |
| | ♣ | | | 1 | 3689 plus 1 strand 554 |
| | | | / | 1 | 413 |

*All backstitching is
done with one strand
**Kreinik Blending Filament

# FRAMES

## MATERIALS & SUPPLIES

(for one frame)

- Cross-stitch fabric
- Fabric scissors
- Frame
- Iron/ironing board
- Mat board (optional)

## INSTRUCTIONS

(for one frame)

1. Stitch desired design.

2. Press, right side down.

3. Cut cross-stitch fabric at least 3" larger on all sides than finished design.

4. Mat and frame finished cross-stitch design as desired.

## STITCHING INFORMATION

Fabric: 28 ct. linen over 2, antique white

Stitch Count: 82w x 110h

Size: 14 count, 5¾" x 7¾"

| XS | SYM | BS | STRANDS | DMC |
|----|-----|----|---------|-----|
| | ⊙ | | 2 | 100 |
| | ⟊ | | 2 | 370 |
| | ɪ | | 2 | 472 |
| | m | | 2 | 518 |
| | ◆ | / | *2 | 562 |
| | ◖ | | 2 | 806 |
| | ∿ | | 2 | 932 |
| | ‡ | | 2 | 989 |
| | ¶ | | 2 | 996 |

*All backstitching is
done with one strand

| XS | SYM | BS | STRANDS | DMC |
|----|-----|----|---------|-----|
| | ◖ | | 2 | 3347 |
| | ■ | | 2 | 3750 |
| | H | | 2 | 3776 |
| | ⋨ | | 2 | 3811 |
| | ↑ | / | *2 | 3826 |
| | ♠ | | 2 | 002 Kreinik Braid #8 |
| | | / | 1 | 317 |
| | | / | 1 | 469 |
| | | / | 1 | 002P Kreinik Cable |

*All backstitching is
done with one strand

Color Variation

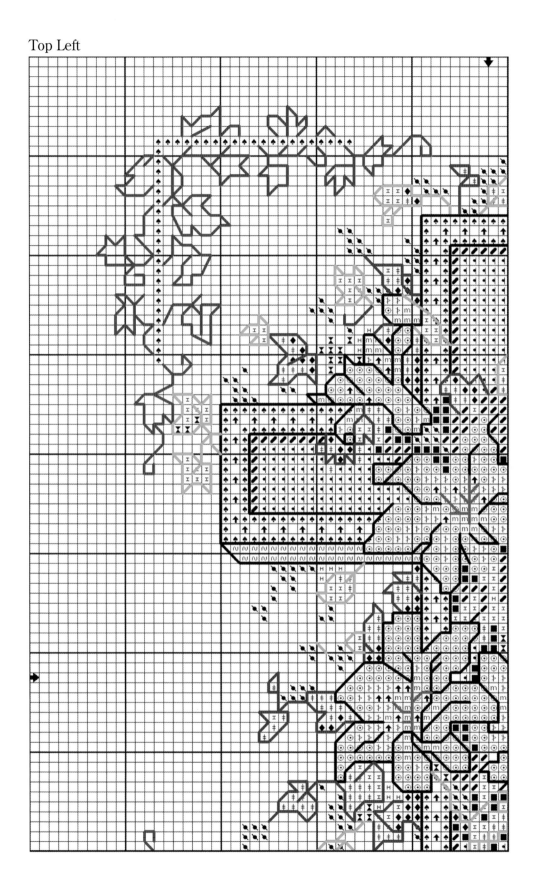

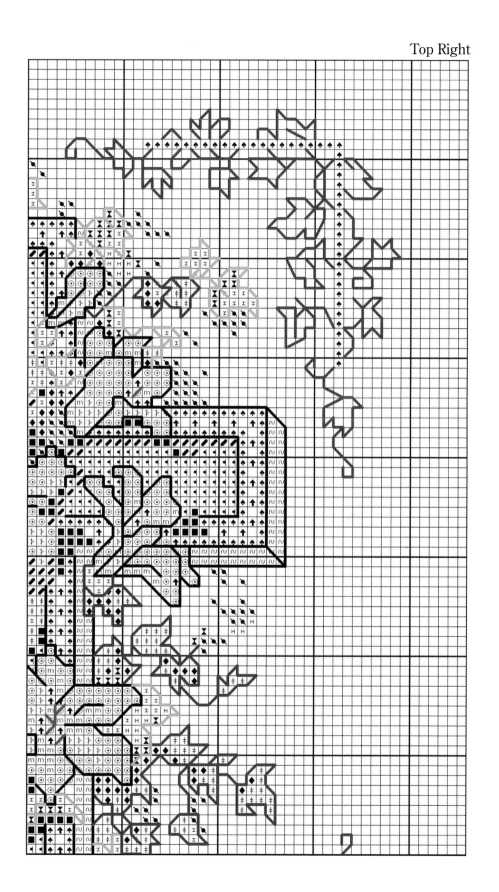

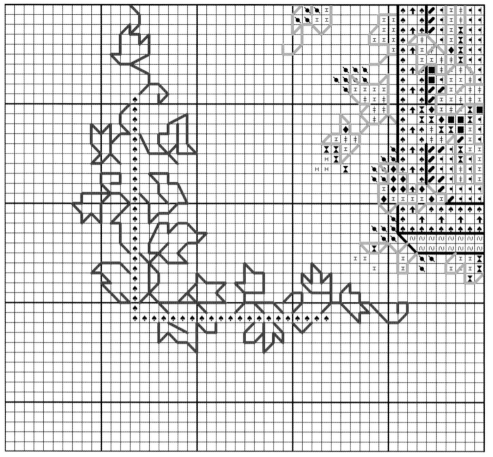

Bottom Left

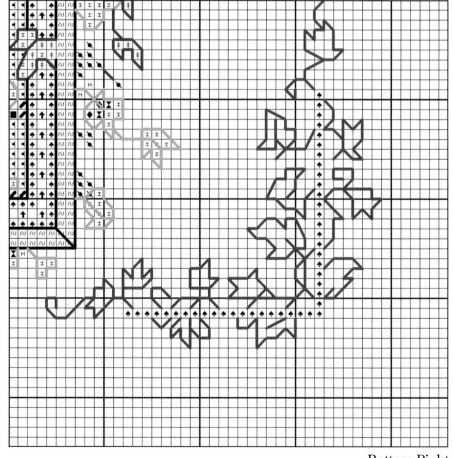

Bottom Right

# CLASSIC DAHLIA

## STITCHING INFORMATION

Fabric: 28ct linen over 2, white

Stitch Count: 194w x 136h

Size: 14 count, 13¾" x 9⅝"

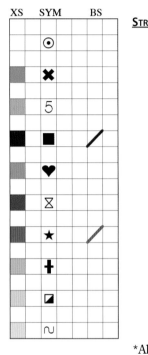
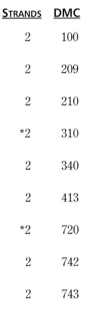

| XS | SYM | BS | STRANDS | DMC |
|---|---|---|---|---|
| | ⊙ | | 2 | 100 |
| | ✖ | | 2 | 209 |
| | 5 | | 2 | 210 |
| | ■ | ╱ | *2 | 310 |
| | ♥ | | 2 | 340 |
| | ⊠ | | 2 | 413 |
| | ★ | ╱ | *2 | 720 |
| | ✝ | | 2 | 742 |
| | ◪ | | 2 | 743 |
| | 2 | | 2 | 744 |

*All backstitching is done with one strand

| XS | SYM | BS | STRANDS | DMC |
|---|---|---|---|---|
| | T | | 2 | 747 |
| | ⊁ | | 2 | 772 |
| | ◕ | ╱ | *2 | 905 |
| | ‡ | | 2 | 970 |
| | ↑ | ╱ | *2 | 986 |
| | n | | 2 | 3347 |
| | ⬡ | | 1 | 895 plus 1 strand 3011 |
| | H | | 1 | 964 plus 1 strand 3813 |
| | ⬭ | | 1 | 958 plus 1 strand 3816 |

*All backstitching is done with one strand

*Color Variation Idea*
*Use floss color of your choice.*

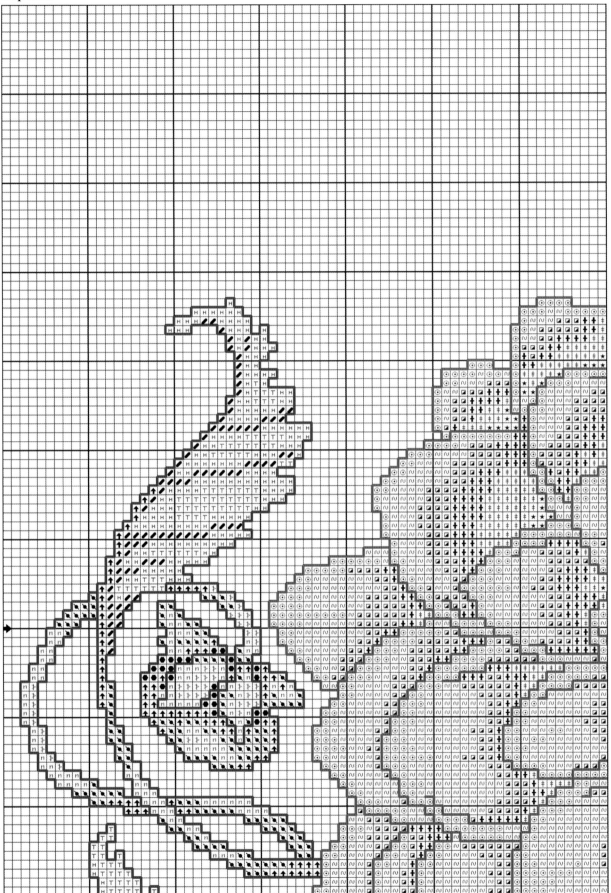

Top Center

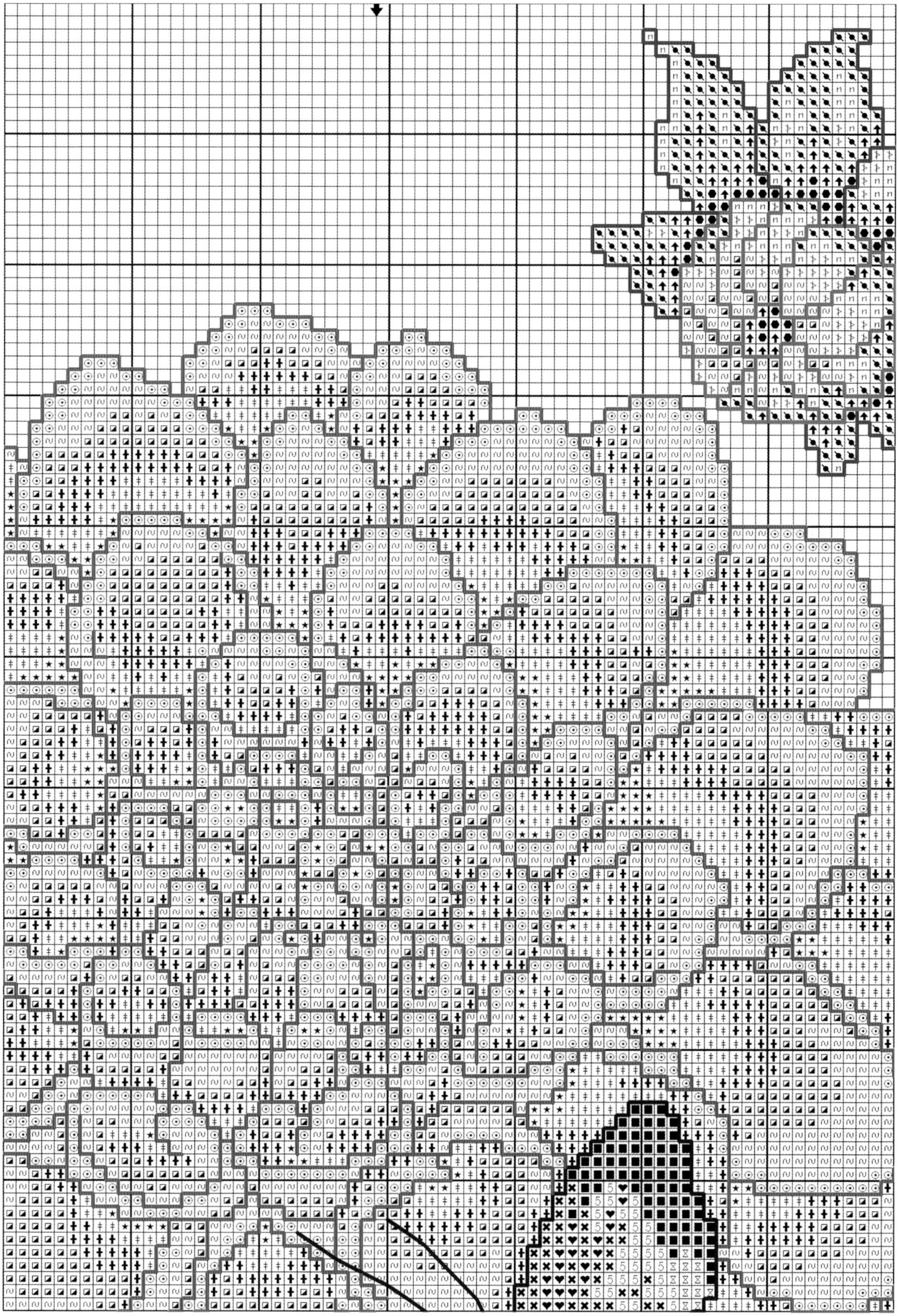

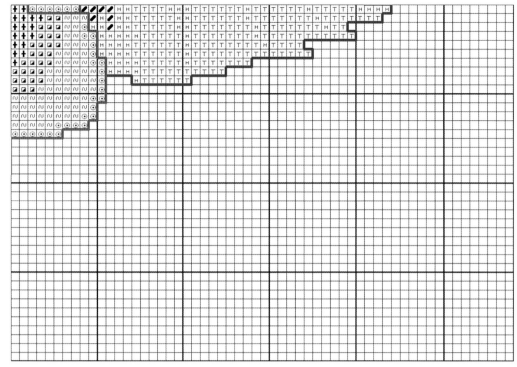

Bottom Right

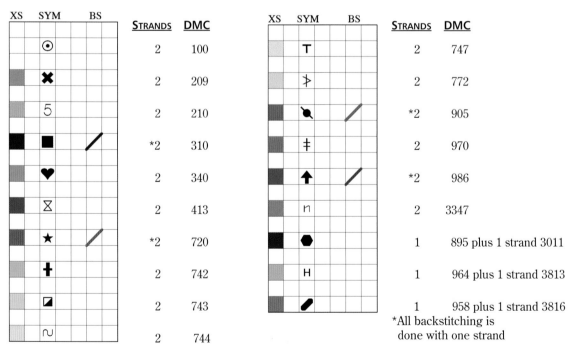

| XS | SYM | BS | Strands | DMC |
|---|---|---|---|---|
| | ⊙ | | 2 | 100 |
| | ✖ | | 2 | 209 |
| | 5 | | 2 | 210 |
| | ■ | / | *2 | 310 |
| | ♥ | | 2 | 340 |
| | ⧖ | | 2 | 413 |
| | ★ | / | *2 | 720 |
| | ✝ | | 2 | 742 |
| | ◪ | | 2 | 743 |
| | ∾ | | 2 | 744 |

*All backstitching is done with one strand

| XS | SYM | BS | Strands | DMC |
|---|---|---|---|---|
| | T | | 2 | 747 |
| | ⊁ | | 2 | 772 |
| | ● | / | *2 | 905 |
| | ǂ | | 2 | 970 |
| | ⬆ | / | *2 | 986 |
| | n | | 2 | 3347 |
| | ⬣ | | 1 | 895 plus 1 strand 3011 |
| | H | | 1 | 964 plus 1 strand 3813 |
| | ⬮ | | 1 | 958 plus 1 strand 3816 |

*All backstitching is done with one strand

# HOME SWEET HOME

## STITCHING INFORMATION

Fabric: Aida 6, beige

Stitch Count: 73w x 59h

Size: 6 count, 12⅛" x 9¾"

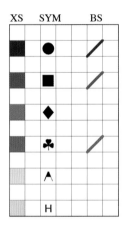

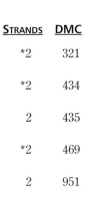

| XS | SYM | BS | STRANDS | DMC |
|----|-----|-----|---------|-----|
| ● | ● | / | *2 | 321 |
| ■ | ■ | / | *2 | 434 |
| ◆ | ◆ | | 2 | 435 |
| ♣ | ♣ | / | *2 | 469 |
| | A | | 2 | 951 |
| | H | | 2 | 963 |

*All backstitching is done with one strand

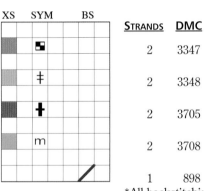

| XS | SYM | BS | STRANDS | DMC |
|----|-----|-----|---------|-----|
| | ▣ | | 2 | 3347 |
| | ‡ | | 2 | 3348 |
| | ✝ | | 2 | 3705 |
| | m | | 2 | 3708 |
| | | / | 1 | 898 |

*All backstitching is done with one strand

*Color Variation Idea*
*Use floss color of your choice.*

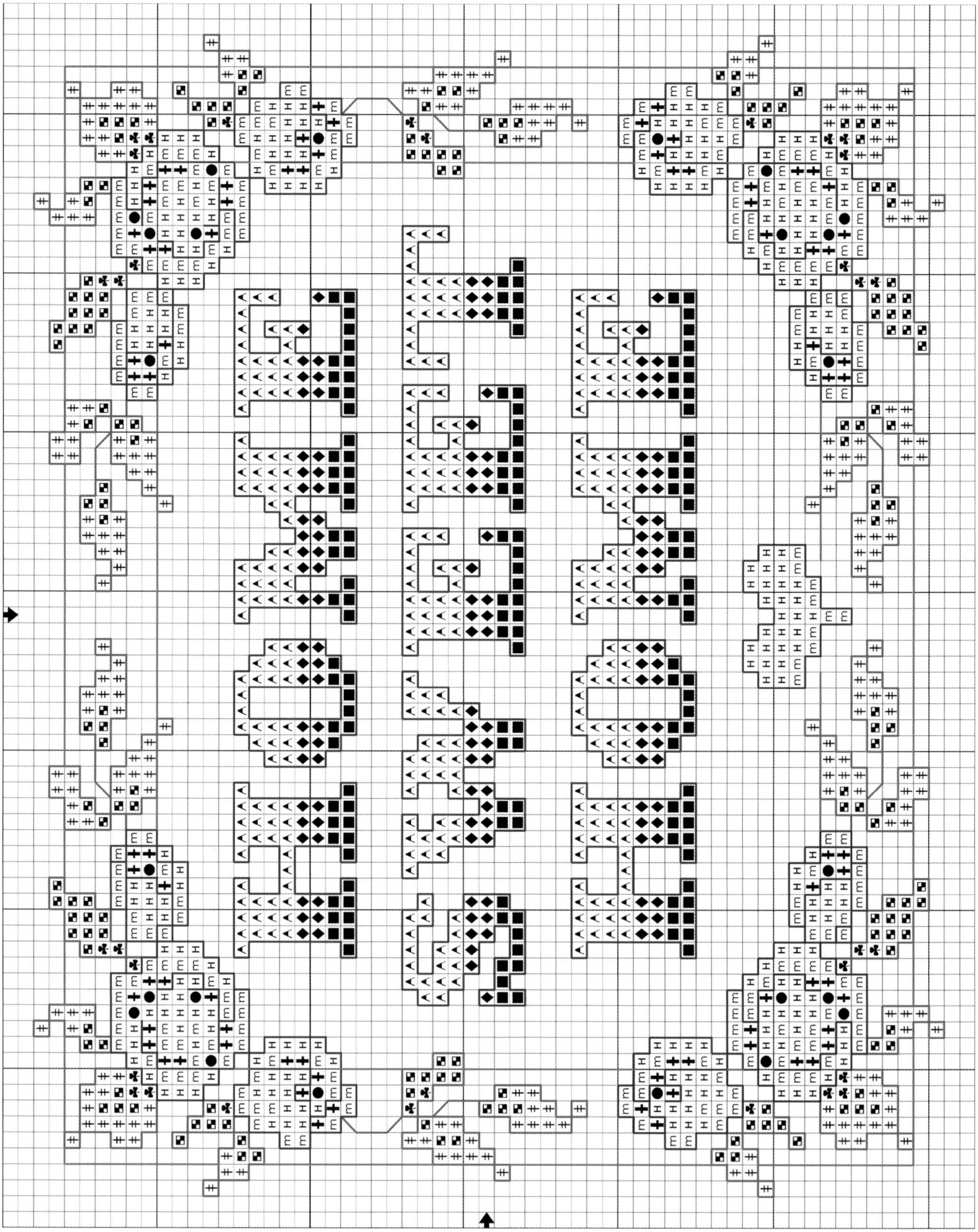

# BLUE BIRD & SUNFLOWER

## STITCHING INFORMATION

Fabric: Aida 14, tea-dyed

Stitch Count: 100w x 103h

Size: 14 count, 7⅛" x 7¼"

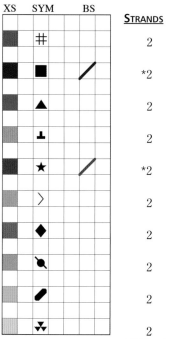

| XS | SYM | BS | STRANDS | DMC |
|----|-----|-----|---------|-----|
| | # | | 2 | 301 |
| | ■ | / | *2 | 310 |
| | ▲ | | 2 | 312 |
| | ⊥ | | 2 | 318 |
| | ★ | / | *2 | 400 |
| | 〉 | | 2 | 402 |
| | ◆ | | 2 | 469 |
| | ◖ | | 2 | 471 |
| | ◖ | | 2 | 742 |
| | ▼▼ | | 2 | 743 |

*All backstitching is
done with one strand

| XS | SYM | BS | STRANDS | DMC |
|----|-----|-----|---------|-----|
| | ∼ | | 2 | 744 |
| | + | | 2 | 800 |
| | ◪ | | 2 | 809 |
| | ↑ | | 2 | 898 |
| | ♥ | | 2 | 947 |
| | ‡ | | 2 | 3341 |
| | 2 | | 2 | 3348 |
| | ⊙ | | 2 | white |
| | | / | 1 | 824 |
| | | / | 1 | 936 |

*All backstitching is
done with one strand

*Color Variation Idea
Use floss color of your choice.*

## STITCHING INFORMATION

Fabric: Aida 14, white

Stitch Count: 45w x 46h

Size: 14 count, 3⅛" x 3¼"

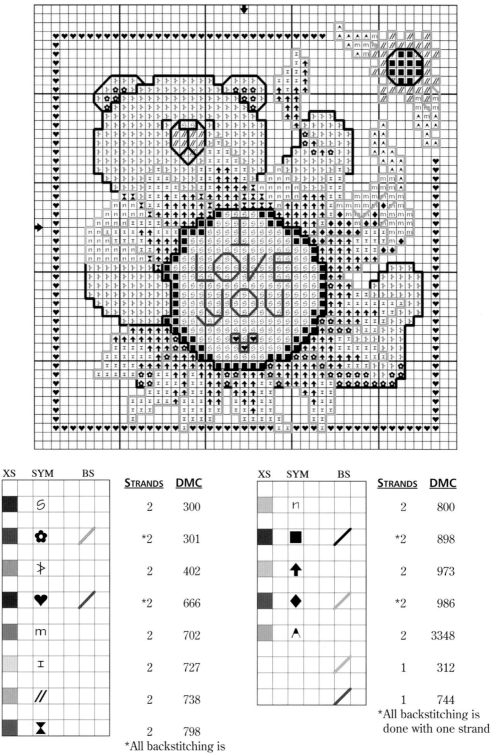

| XS | SYM | BS | STRANDS | DMC |
|---|---|---|---|---|
| | S | | 2 | 300 |
| | ✿ | / | *2 | 301 |
| | ⊁ | | 2 | 402 |
| | ♥ | / | *2 | 666 |
| | m | | 2 | 702 |
| | I | | 2 | 727 |
| | // | | 2 | 738 |
| | ✕ | | 2 | 798 |

*All backstitching is done with one strand

| XS | SYM | BS | STRANDS | DMC |
|---|---|---|---|---|
| | n | | 2 | 800 |
| | ■ | / | *2 | 898 |
| | ↑ | | 2 | 973 |
| | ◆ | / | *2 | 986 |
| | ∧ | | 2 | 3348 |
| | | / | 1 | 312 |
| | | / | 1 | 744 |

*All backstitching is done with one strand

# SUNFLOWER SEEDS

## STITCHING INFORMATION

Fabric: Aida 14, black

Stitch Count: 53w x 65h

Size: 14 count, 3¾" x 4⅝"

| XS | SYM | QS | BS | STRANDS | DMC |
|---|---|---|---|---|---|
|  | ▣ |  |  | 2 | 301 |
|  | ⬆ |  | ╱ | *2 | 400 |
|  | n |  |  | 2 | 402 |
|  | ◆ |  | ╱ | *2 | 469 |
|  | ▬ |  |  | 2 | 721 |
|  | ⊙ |  |  | 2 | 742 |
|  | H |  |  | 2 | 744 |
|  | ■ |  | ╱ | *2 | 798 |

*All backstitching is done with one strand

| XS | SYM | QS | BS | STRANDS | DMC |
|---|---|---|---|---|---|
|  | ✚ |  |  | 2 | 798 |
|  | I | ɪ |  | 2 | 800 |
|  | ◈ |  |  | 2 | 809 |
|  | ♥ |  |  | 2 | 918 |
|  | ✛ |  |  | 2 | 3347 |
|  | a | a |  | 2 | 3348 |
|  |  |  | ╱ | 1 | 310 |

*All backstitching is done with one strand

# MAGNIFICENT IRIS

## STITCHING INFORMATION

Fabric: 28ct. linen over 2, white

Stitch Count: 122w x 125h

Size: 14 count, 8⅝" x 8⅞"

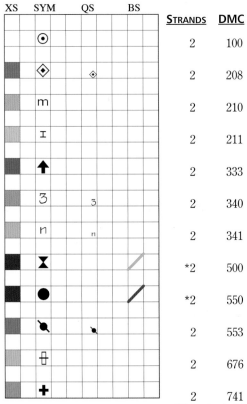

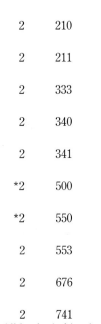

| XS | SYM | QS | BS | STRANDS | DMC |
|----|-----|-----|-----|---------|-----|
| | ⊙ | | | 2 | 100 |
| | ◈ | ◈ | | 2 | 208 |
| | m | | | 2 | 210 |
| | ɪ | | | 2 | 211 |
| | ♠ | | | 2 | 333 |
| | 3 | 3 | | 2 | 340 |
| | n | n | | 2 | 341 |
| | ✗ | | / | *2 | 500 |
| | ● | | / | *2 | 550 |
| | ◣ | ◣ | | 2 | 553 |
| | ⊟ | | | 2 | 676 |
| | ✚ | | | 2 | 741 |

*All backstitching is done with one strand

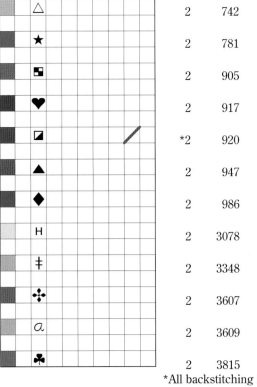

| XS | SYM | QS | BS | STRANDS | DMC |
|----|-----|-----|-----|---------|-----|
| | △ | | | 2 | 742 |
| | ★ | | | 2 | 781 |
| | ▣ | | | 2 | 905 |
| | ♥ | | | 2 | 917 |
| | ◪ | | / | *2 | 920 |
| | ▲ | | | 2 | 947 |
| | ◆ | | | 2 | 986 |
| | H | | | 2 | 3078 |
| | ‡ | | | 2 | 3348 |
| | ✜ | | | 2 | 3607 |
| | a | | | 2 | 3609 |
| | ♣ | | | 2 | 3815 |

*All backstitching is done with one strand

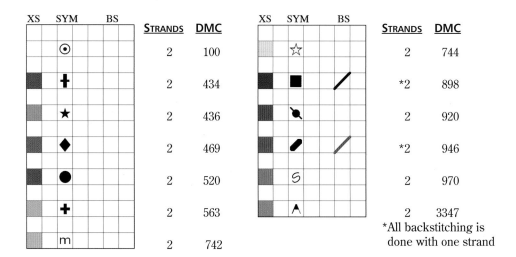

Bottom Left

Bottom Right

| XS | SYM | BS | STRANDS | DMC |
|---|---|---|---|---|
| | ⊙ | | 2 | 100 |
| | ✛ | | 2 | 434 |
| | ★ | | 2 | 436 |
| | ◆ | | 2 | 469 |
| | ● | | 2 | 520 |
| | ✚ | | 2 | 563 |
| | m | | 2 | 742 |

| XS | SYM | BS | STRANDS | DMC |
|---|---|---|---|---|
| | ☆ | | 2 | 744 |
| | ■ | ╱ | *2 | 898 |
| | ◖ | | 2 | 920 |
| | ◗ | ╱ | *2 | 946 |
| | S | | 2 | 970 |
| | ∧ | | 2 | 3347 |

*All backstitching is done with one strand

60

# ALLURING AMARYLLIS

## STITCHING INFORMATION

Fabric: 28ct linen over 2, white

Stitch Count: 131w x 185h

Size: 14 count, 9¼" x 13⅛"

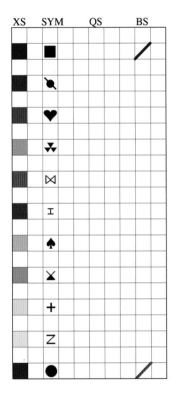

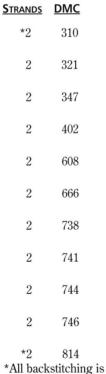

| STRANDS | DMC |
|---|---|
| *2 | 310 |
| 2 | 321 |
| 2 | 347 |
| 2 | 402 |
| 2 | 608 |
| 2 | 666 |
| 2 | 738 |
| 2 | 741 |
| 2 | 744 |
| 2 | 746 |
| *2 | 814 |

*All backstitching is
done with one strand

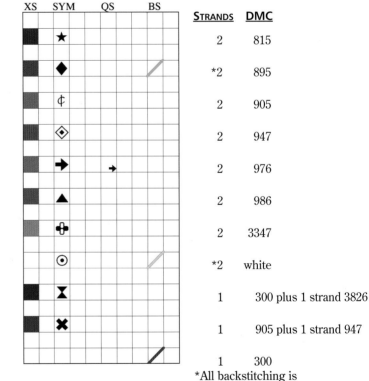

| STRANDS | DMC |
|---|---|
| 2 | 815 |
| *2 | 895 |
| 2 | 905 |
| 2 | 947 |
| 2 | 976 |
| 2 | 986 |
| 2 | 3347 |
| *2 | white |
| 1 | 300 plus 1 strand 3826 |
| 1 | 905 plus 1 strand 947 |
| 1 | 300 |

*All backstitching is
done with one strand

Top Left

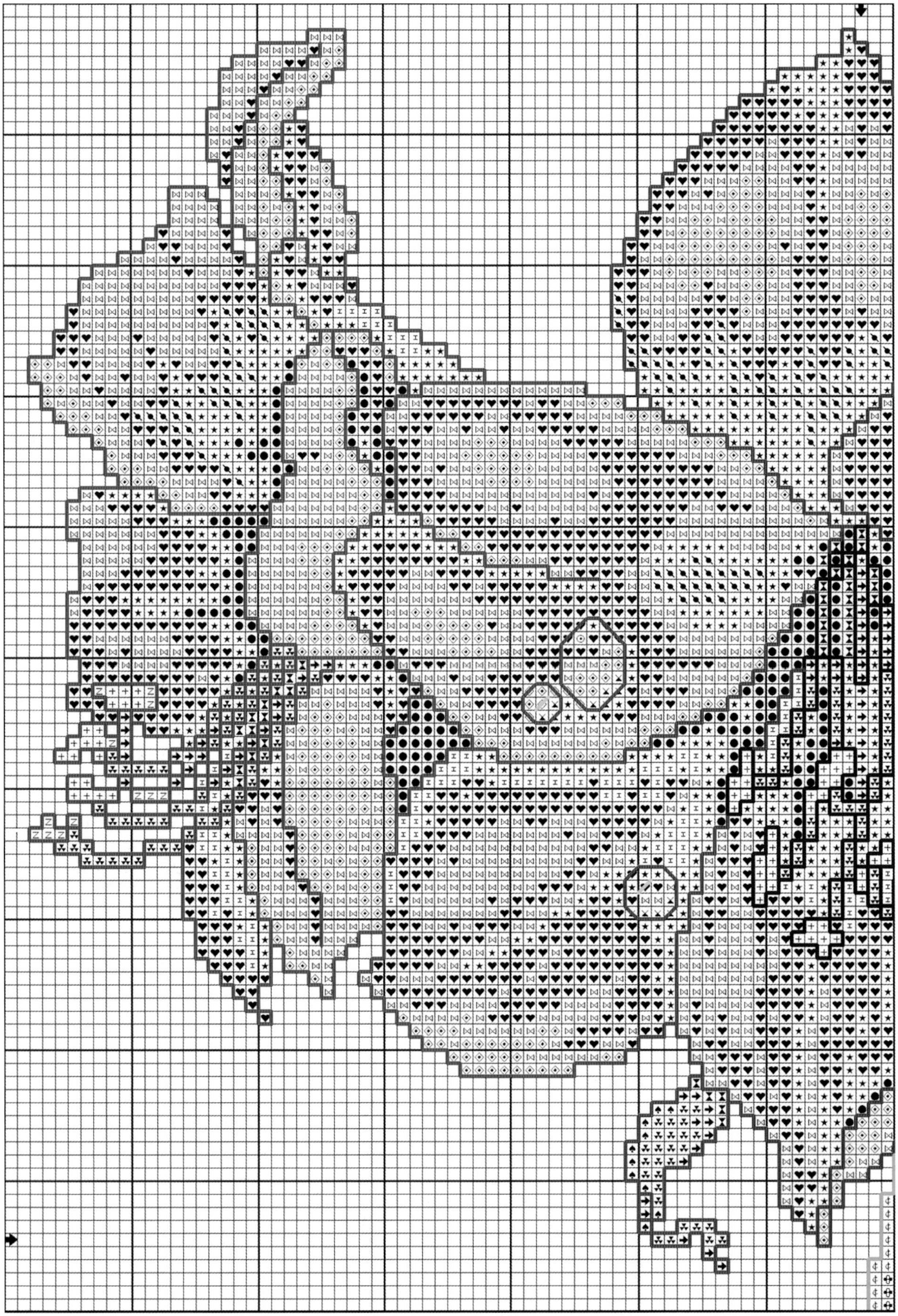

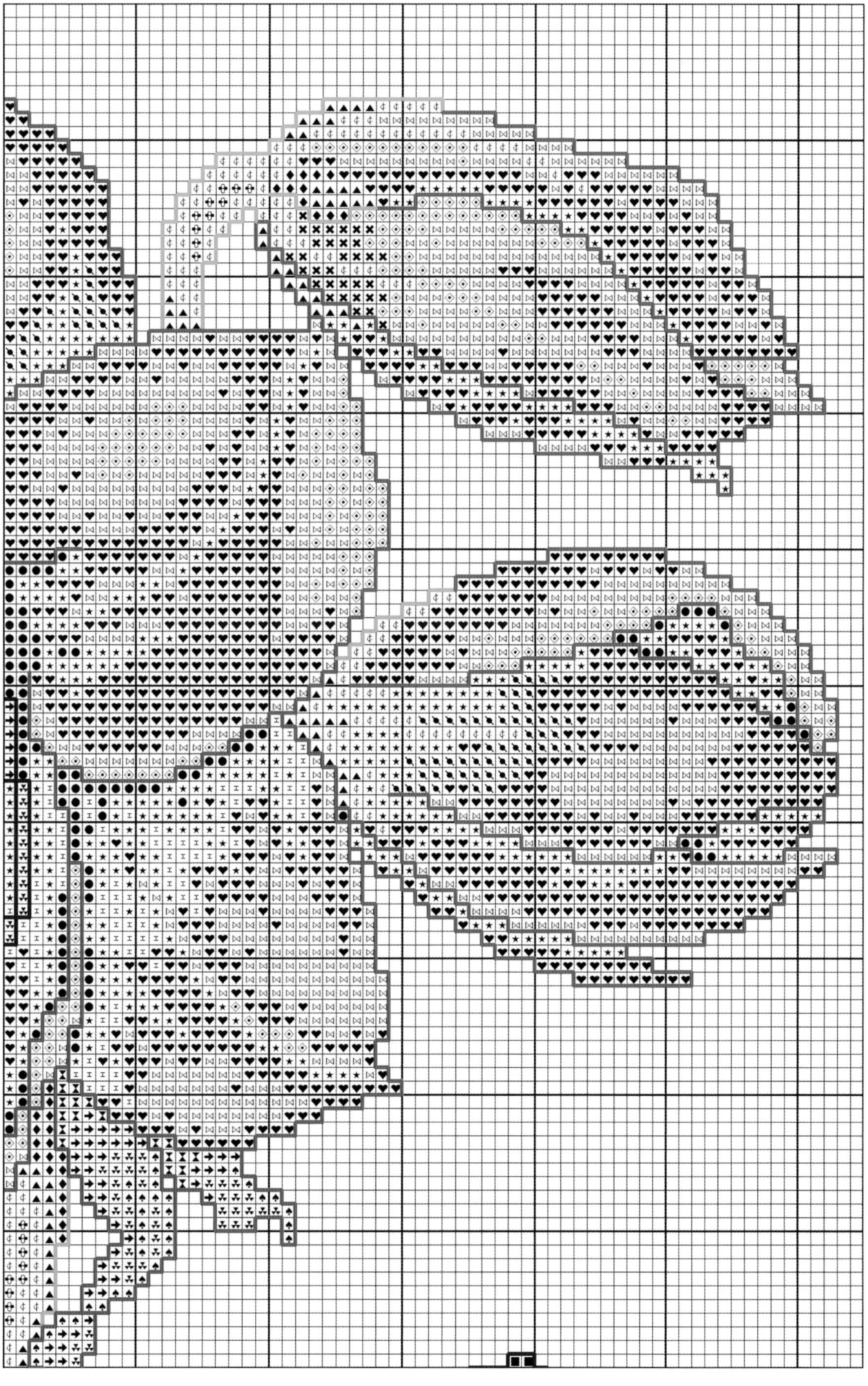

Bottom Left

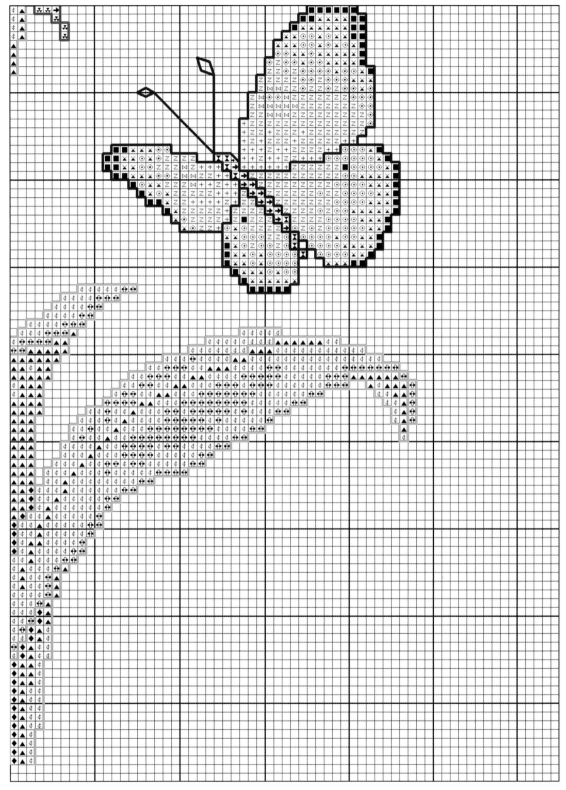

Bottom Right

# FLOWER GARDEN FAIRY

## STITCHING INFORMATION

Fabric: Aida 14, white

Stitch Count: 132w x 175h

Size: 14 count, 9⅜" x 12½"

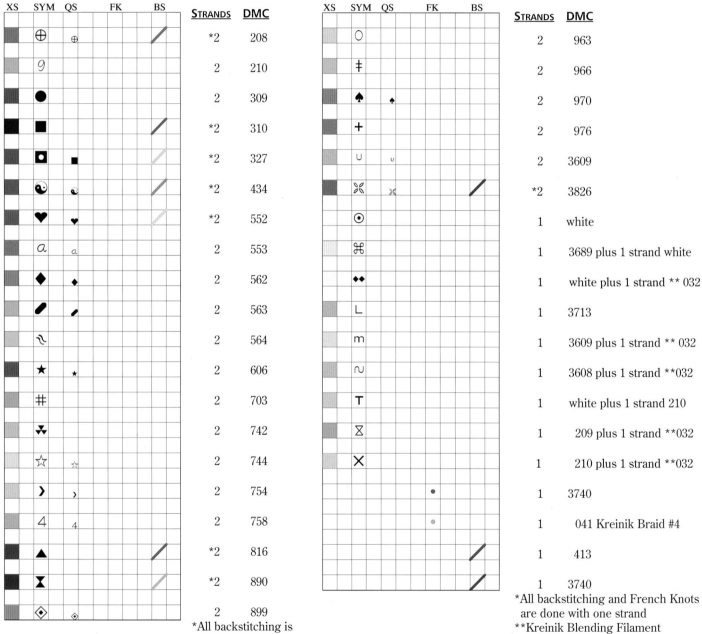

| XS | SYM | QS | FK | BS | STRANDS | DMC |
|---|---|---|---|---|---|---|
|  | ⊕ | ⊕ |  | / | *2 | 208 |
|  | 9 |  |  |  | 2 | 210 |
|  | ● |  |  |  | 2 | 309 |
|  | ■ |  |  | / | *2 | 310 |
|  | ▣ | ■ |  | / | *2 | 327 |
|  | ☯ | ☯ |  | / | *2 | 434 |
|  | ♥ | ♥ |  | / | *2 | 552 |
|  | a | a |  |  | 2 | 553 |
|  | ◆ | ◆ |  |  | 2 | 562 |
|  | ✎ | ✎ |  |  | 2 | 563 |
|  | ~ |  |  |  | 2 | 564 |
|  | ★ | ★ |  |  | 2 | 606 |
|  | # |  |  |  | 2 | 703 |
|  | ❦ |  |  |  | 2 | 742 |
|  | ☆ | ☆ |  |  | 2 | 744 |
|  | ❭ | ❭ |  |  | 2 | 754 |
|  | 4 | 4 |  |  | 2 | 758 |
|  | ▲ |  |  | / | *2 | 816 |
|  | ✕ |  |  | / | *2 | 890 |
|  | ◈ | ◈ |  |  | 2 | 899 |

*All backstitching is
done with one strand

| XS | SYM | QS | FK | BS | STRANDS | DMC |
|---|---|---|---|---|---|---|
|  | ○ |  |  |  | 2 | 963 |
|  | ‡ |  |  |  | 2 | 966 |
|  | ♠ | ♠ |  |  | 2 | 970 |
|  | ✛ |  |  |  | 2 | 976 |
|  | ∪ | ∪ |  |  | 2 | 3609 |
|  | ✾ | ✾ |  | / | *2 | 3826 |
|  | ⊙ |  |  |  | 1 | white |
|  | ⌘ |  |  |  | 1 | 3689 plus 1 strand white |
|  | ◆◆ |  |  |  | 1 | white plus 1 strand ** 032 |
|  | L |  |  |  | 1 | 3713 |
|  | m |  |  |  | 1 | 3609 plus 1 strand ** 032 |
|  | ∾ |  |  |  | 1 | 3608 plus 1 strand **032 |
|  | T |  |  |  | 1 | white plus 1 strand 210 |
|  | ⊠ |  |  |  | 1 | 209 plus 1 strand **032 |
|  | ✕ |  |  |  | 1 | 210 plus 1 strand **032 |
|  |  |  | ● |  | 1 | 3740 |
|  |  |  | ● |  | 1 | 041 Kreinik Braid #4 |
|  |  |  |  | / | 1 | 413 |
|  |  |  |  | / | 1 | 3740 |

*All backstitching and French Knots
are done with one strand
**Kreinik Blending Filament

68

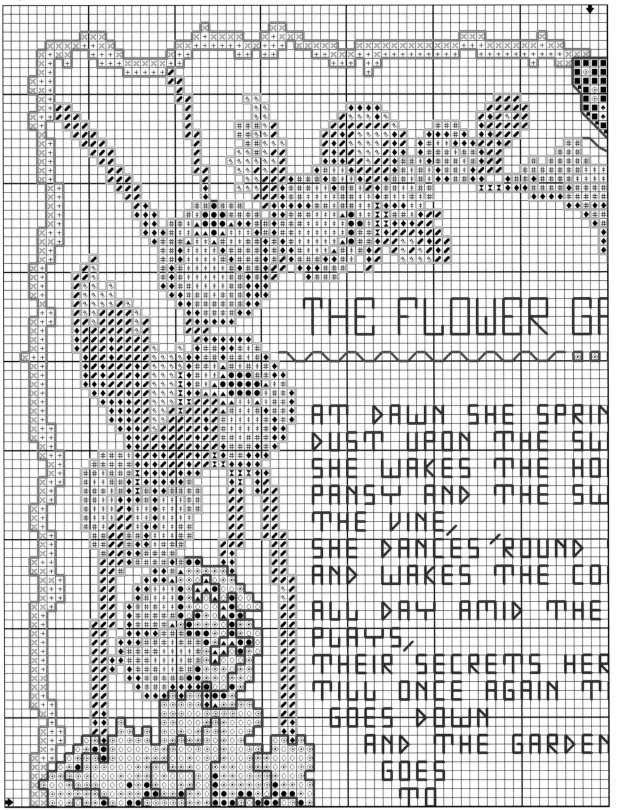

THE FLOWER GA

AT DAWN SHE SPRIN
DUST UPON THE SL
SHE WAKES THE HO
PANSY AND THE SL
THE VINE,
SHE DANCES 'ROUND
AND WAKES THE CO
ALL DAY AMID THE
PLAYS,
THEIR SECRETS HER
TILL ONCE AGAIN T
GOES DOWN
AND THE GARDEN
GOES
TO

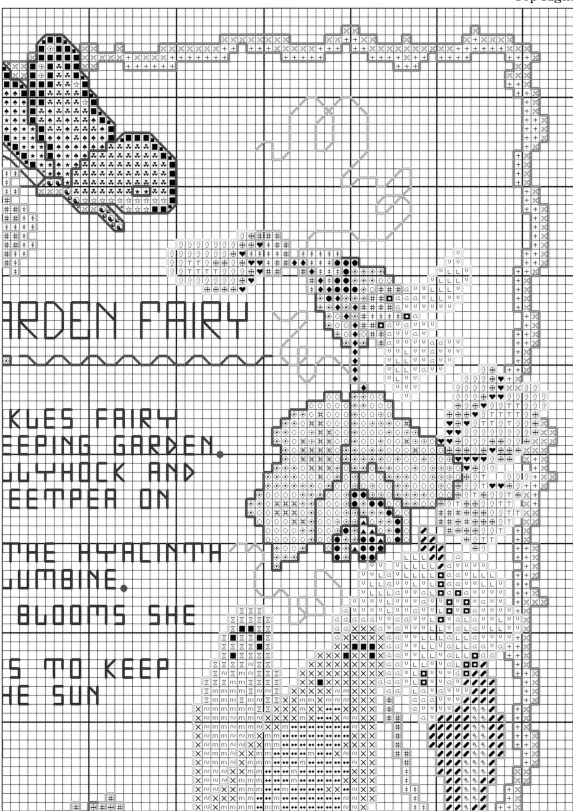

ARDEN FAIRY

KLES FAIRY
EEPING GARDEN.
JLYHOCK AND
EETPEA ON

THE HYACINTH
JUMBINE.
BLOOMS SHE

S TO KEEP
HE SUN

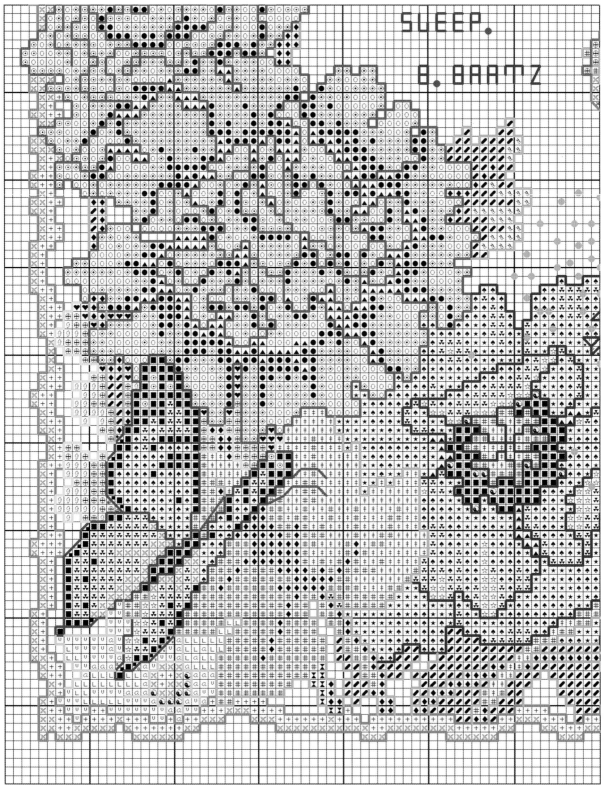

Bottom Left

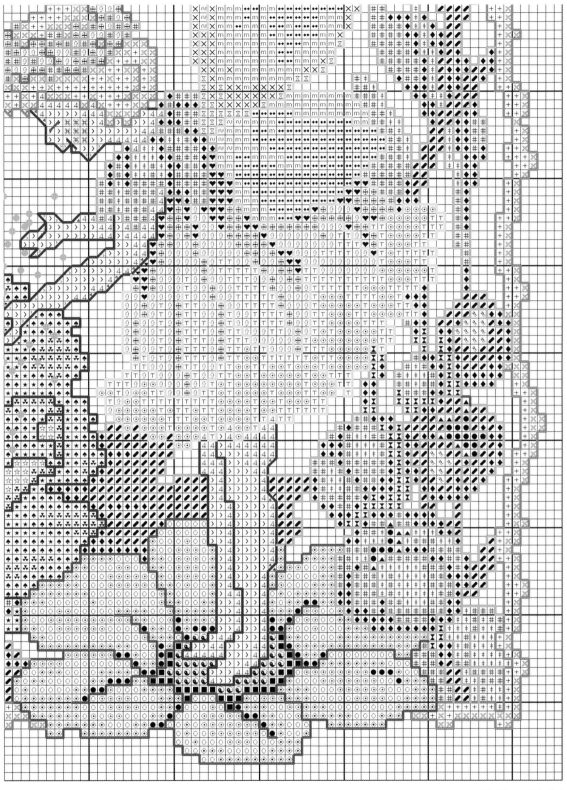

Bottom Right

# LUSCIOUS TREE PEONY

## STITCHING INFORMATION

Fabric: 28 ct. linen over 2, white

Stitch Count: 192w x 123h

Size: 14 count, 13⅝" x 8¾"

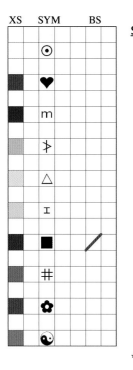

| XS | SYM | BS | STRANDS | DMC |
|---|---|---|---|---|
|  | ⊙ |  | 2 | 100 |
|  | ♥ |  | 2 | 309 |
|  | m |  | 2 | 321 |
|  | ⚡ |  | 2 | 605 |
|  | △ |  | 2 | 747 |
|  | I |  | 2 | 772 |
|  | ■ | / | *2 | 815 |
|  | # |  | 2 | 905 |
|  | ✿ |  | 2 | 920 |
|  | ☯ |  | 2 | 922 |

*All backstitching is
done with one strand

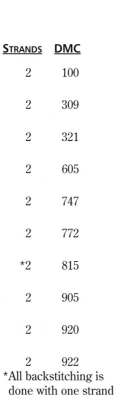

| XS | SYM | BS | STRANDS | DMC |
|---|---|---|---|---|
|  | a |  | 2 | 956 |
|  | + |  | 2 | 977 |
|  | ➜ |  | 2 | 986 |
|  | ◇ |  | 2 | 3347 |
|  | H |  | 2 | 3689 |
|  | ☆ |  | 2 | 3827 |
|  | ◆ |  | 1 | 895  plus 1 strand 3011 |
|  | ∿ |  | 1 | 964  plus 1 strand 3813 |
|  | ♠ |  | 1 | 958 plus 1 strand 3816 |
|  |  | / | 1 | 895 |

*All backstitching is
done with one strand

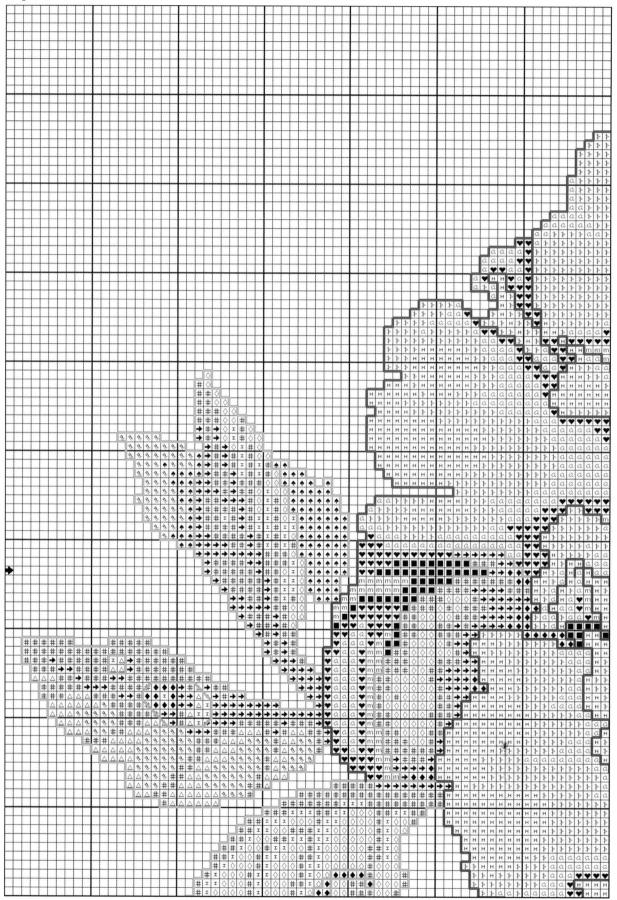

Center

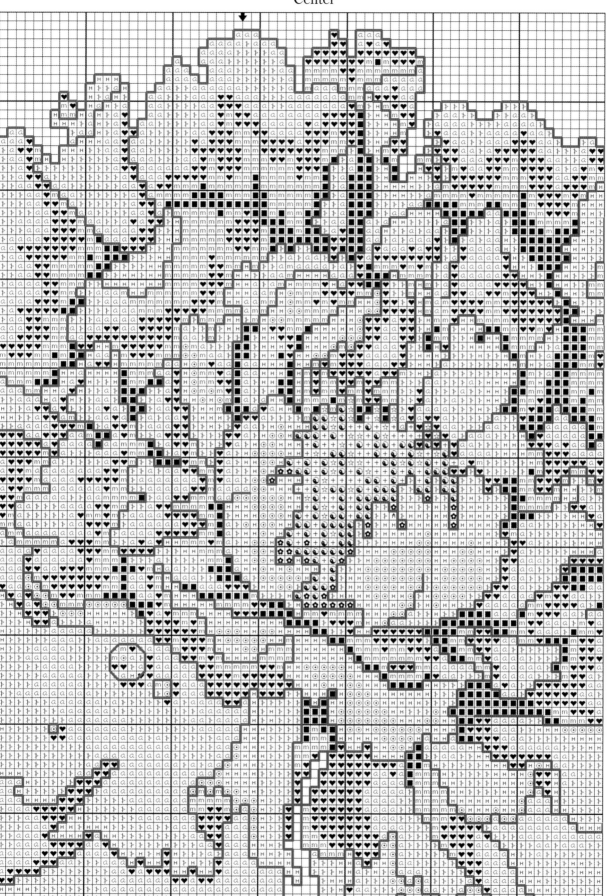

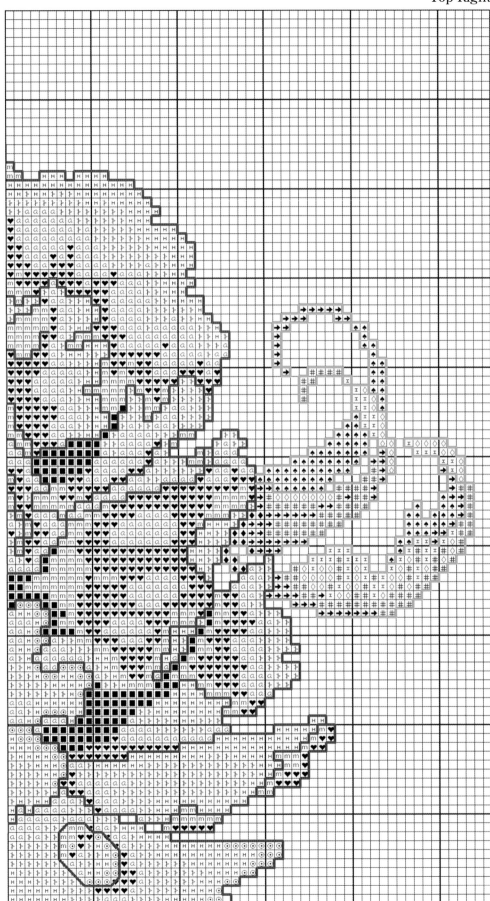

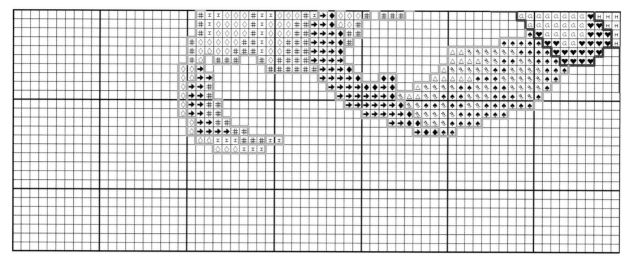

Bottom Left

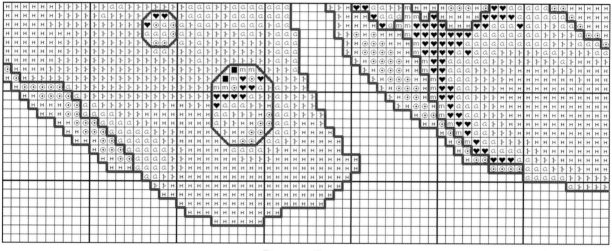

Bottom Center

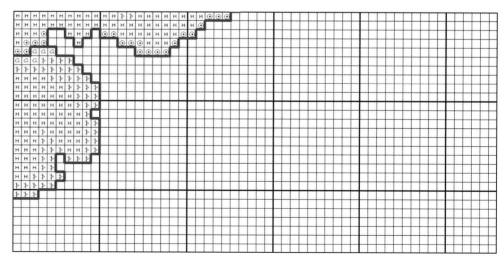

Bottom Right

# PURSES

## MATERIALS & SUPPLIES

(for one purse)

- Desired Aida 14 cross-stitch fabric
- Fabric hoop
- Fabric scissors
- Felt for lining
- Iron/ironing board
- Pencil
- Purse clasp
- Sewing needle
- Sewing thread to match fabric
- Straight pins
- Tracing paper

## INSTRUCTIONS

(for one purse)

1. With fabric in hoop, stitch desired design.

2. Remove cross-stitched piece from fabric hoop. Press, right side down.

3. Using a pencil, trace desired purse pattern onto tracing paper. See pages 121–122.

4. Place stitched front and back with wrong sides together. Pin traced pattern centered over stitched front. Cut out front and back, then repeat with two pieces of felt for lining.

5. Place front and back with right sides together and stitch from X down around bottom to X with a ¼" seam allowance. Clip curves. Turn purse and gently press seam. If necessary, reinforce seam with a few tack stitches at start and end of stitching.

6. Stitch felt lining pieces from * to * shown on purse pattern with a ⅜" seam allowance. Trim close to stitching. Insert lining into purse. Align top raw edges of purse and lining and baste together. Refer to Baste on page 6.

7. Insert top edges of purse/lining up into purse clasp, using one of the following methods:

   a. For Evening Thistle, Butterfly Charmer, and Flowers & Lace: Use six strands of floss, sew edges of purse/lining to holes in clasp as shown on individual project patterns. Do not carry floss across hinges.

   b. For Almost Real Rose, Sunflower Meeting, and Three Butterflies: Use six strands of floss, sew edges of purse/lining to holes in clasp as shown on individual project patterns. Do not carry floss across hinges.

8. Add chain and tassels as desired.

# EVENING THISTLE

## STITCHING INFORMATION

Fabric: Aida 14, black

Stitch Count: 59w x 64h

Size: 14 count, 4⅛" x 4½"

Purse Pattern on page 121

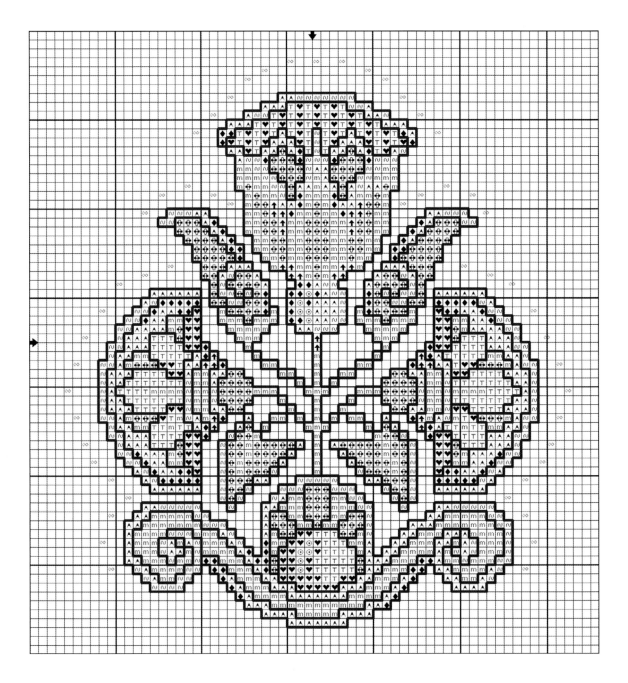

| XS | SYM | BS | | STRANDS | DMC |
|----|-----|----|----|---------|-----|
| | ⊙ | | | 2 | white |
| | ◆ | | | 2 | 301 |
| | ♥ | | | 2 | 309 |
| | Λ | | | 2 | 402 |
| | ↑ | | | 2 | 469 |
| | ∪ | | | 2 | 745 |
| | T | | | 2 | 956 |
| | ✛ | | | 2 | 993 |
| | m | | | 2 | 3347 |
| | ◇◇ | | | 2 | **02011 |
| | | / | | 1 | 310 |

**Mill Hill GS Bead

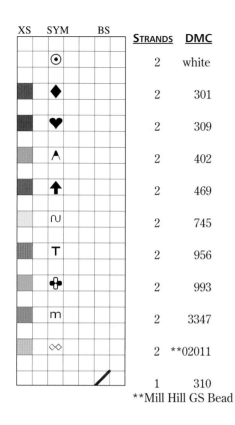

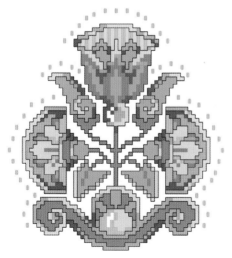

Color Variation Idea
Use floss color of your choice.

# BUTTERFLY CHARMER

## STITCHING INFORMATION

Fabric: 28 ct. linen over 2, ivory

Stitch Count: 60w x 64h

Size: 14 count, 4¼" x 4½"

Purse Pattern on page 121

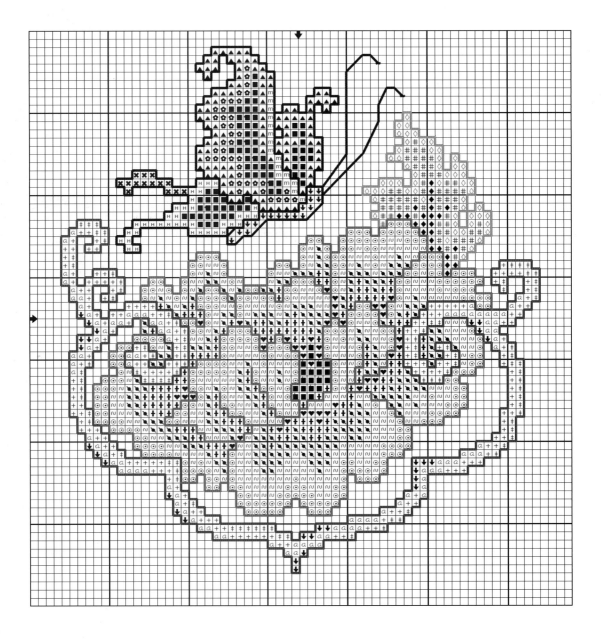

| XS | SYM | BS | STRANDS | DMC |
|----|-----|----|---------|-----|
|  | ⊙ |  | 2 | white |
|  | ✖ |  | 2 | 208 |
|  | H |  | 2 | 209 |
|  | ✚ | / | *2 | 309 |
|  | ■ | / | *2 | 310 |
|  | ◆ | / | *2 | 501 |
|  | # |  | 2 | 503 |
|  | + |  | 2 | 741 |
|  | ‡ |  | 2 | 744 |
|  | ▲ |  | 2 | 798 |
|  | m |  | 2 | 809 |
|  | ♥ |  | 2 | 814 |
|  | ◇ |  | 2 | 834 |
|  | ◖ |  | 2 | 899 |
|  | ✦ | / | *2 | 920 |
|  | a |  | 2 | 947 |
|  | ✿ |  | 2 | 958 |
|  | ∿ |  | 2 | 963 |
|  | ◆◆ |  |  | **02008 |
|  | $ |  |  | **02011 |

*All backstitching is
 done with one strand
**Mill Hill GS Bead

# SUNFLOWER MEETING

## STITCHING INFORMATION

Fabric: Aida 14, white

Stitch Count: 47w x 57h

Size: 14 count, 3¼" x 4"

Purse Pattern on page 122

| XS | SYM | FK | BS | STRANDS | DMC |
|----|-----|----|----|---------|-----|
| | ⊙ | | | 2 | 1 |
| ■ | ■ | | ╱ | *2 | 310 |
| | m | | | 2 | 321 |
| | H | | | 2 | 606 |
| | a | | | 2 | 741 |
| | 2 | | | 2 | 744 |
| | ♥ | | | 2 | 815 |
| | ⊙ | | | 2 | 920 |
| | ◆ | | | 2 | 937 |
| | ★ | | | 2 | 947 |
| | ♣ | | | 2 | 3347 |
| | I | | | 2 | 3364 |
| | | • | | 1 | **12207 |

*All backstitching is
done with one strand
**Mill Hill Fluted
Heart Custom Bead

Color Variation Idea
Use floss color of your choice.

# ALMOST REAL ROSE

### STITCHING INFORMATION

Fabric: Aida 14, white

Stitch Count: 53w x 58h

Size: 14 count, 3¾" x 4⅛"

Purse Pattern on page 122

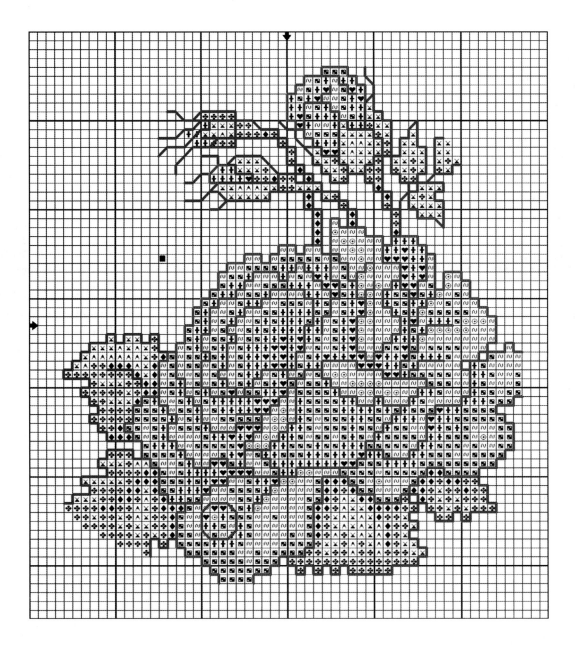

| XS | SYM | BS | STRANDS | DMC |
|---|---|---|---|---|
|  | ⊙ |  | 2 | 1 |
|  | ✚ | / | *2 | 309 |
|  | ♣ |  | 2 | 469 |
|  | ∧ |  | 2 | 772 |
|  | ♥ |  | 2 | 814 |

*All backstitching is
done with one strand

| XS | SYM | BS | STRANDS | DMC |
|---|---|---|---|---|
|  | ◨ |  | 2 | 899 |
|  | ◆ | / | *2 | 936 |
|  | ∽ |  | 2 | 963 |
|  | ✖ |  | 2 | 3347 |
|  | ■ |  | 2 | **12204 |

*All backstitching is
done with one strand
**Mill Hill Custom Bead

## STITCHING INFORMATION

Fabric: Aida 14, white

Stitch Count: 43w x 58h

Size: 14 count, 3" x 4⅛"

Purse Pattern on page 121

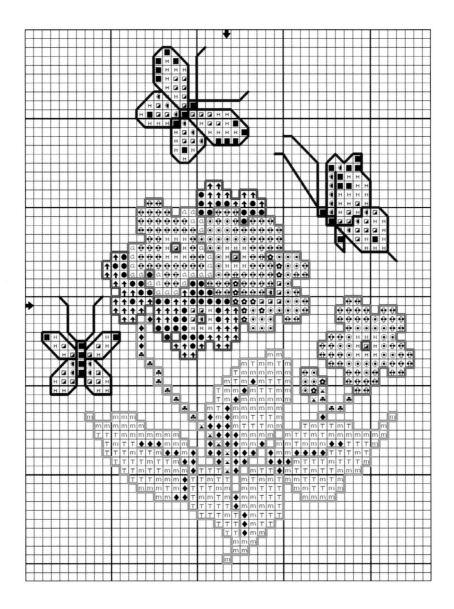

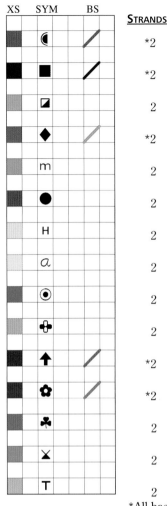

| XS | SYM | BS | STRANDS | DMC |
|----|-----|-----|---------|-----|
| | ◖ | / | *2 | 301 |
| | ■ | / | *2 | 310 |
| | ◪ | | 2 | 402 |
| | ◆ | / | *2 | 501 |
| | m | | 2 | 503 |
| | ● | | 2 | 718 |
| | H | | 2 | 744 |
| | a | | 2 | 775 |
| | ◉ | | 2 | 798 |
| | ✚ | | 2 | 809 |
| | ↑ | / | *2 | 814 |
| | ✿ | / | *2 | 820 |
| | ♣ | | 2 | 905 |
| | ✖ | | 2 | 3347 |
| | T | | 2 | 3813 |

*All backstitching is
done with one strand

Color Variation Idea
Use floss color of your choice.

# FLOWERS & LACE

## STITCHING INFORMATION

Fabric: Aida 14, dirty

Stitch Count: 63w x 80h

Size: 14 count, 4½" x 5⅝"

Purse Pattern on page 121

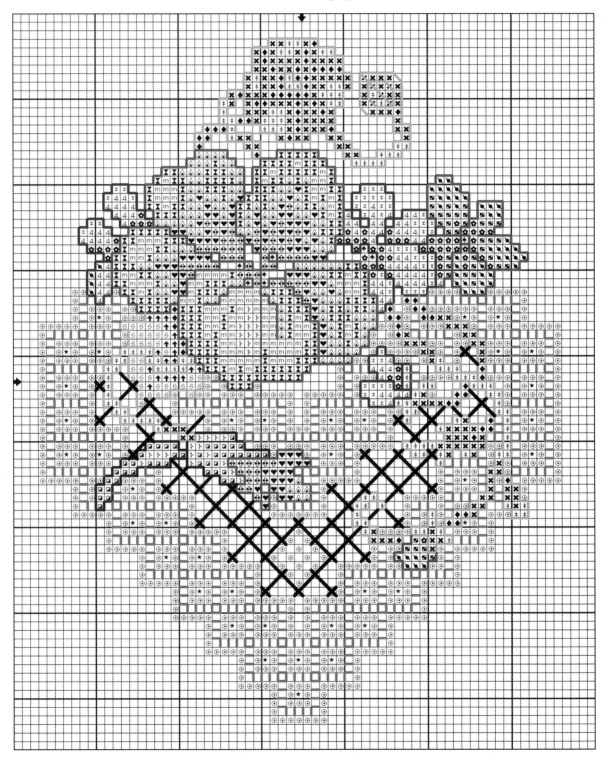

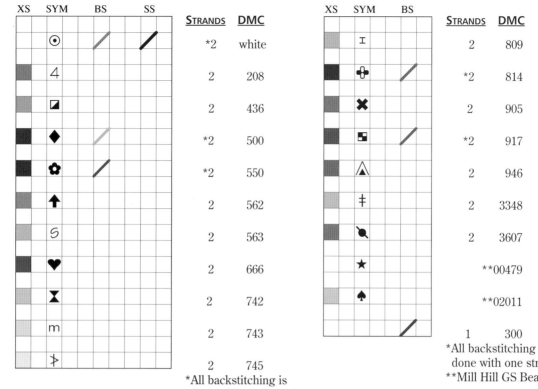

| XS | SYM | BS | SS | STRANDS | DMC |
|----|-----|----|----|---------|-----|
| | ⊙ | / | / | *2 | white |
| | 4 | | | 2 | 208 |
| | ◩ | | | 2 | 436 |
| | ◆ | / | | *2 | 500 |
| | ✿ | / | | *2 | 550 |
| | ↑ | | | 2 | 562 |
| | S | | | 2 | 563 |
| | ♥ | | | 2 | 666 |
| | ⏳ | | | 2 | 742 |
| | m | | | 2 | 743 |
| | ⟩ | | | 2 | 745 |

*All backstitching is done with one strand

| XS | SYM | BS | STRANDS | DMC |
|----|-----|----|---------|-----|
| | I | | 2 | 809 |
| | ✛ | / | *2 | 814 |
| | ✖ | | 2 | 905 |
| | ◧ | / | *2 | 917 |
| | △ | | 2 | 946 |
| | ‡ | | 2 | 3348 |
| | ◗ | | 2 | 3607 |
| | ★ | | | **00479 |
| | ♠ | | | **02011 |
| | | / | 1 | 300 |

*All backstitching is done with one strand
**Mill Hill GS Bead

# PILLOWS

## MATERIALS & SUPPLIES
(for one pillow)

- Batting
- Binding fabric (¼ yd)
- Desired even-weave cross-stitch fabric
- Fabric hoop
- Fabric scissors
- Iron/ironing board
- Pillow fabric (¾ yd)
- Sewing needle
- Sewing thread to match fabric
- Straight pins
- Tape measure

## INSTRUCTIONS
(for one pillow)

1. With fabric in hoop, stitch desired design. Refer to individual project instructions before beginning Step 2.

2. Remove finished cross-stitched piece from fabric hoop. Press, right side down.

3. Trim cross-stitched piece to 1¾" beyond design on all sides. Zigzag or serge raw edge. With right sides together and matching edges, sew a short border strip to each side of the cross-stitched piece. Press seam toward border. Repeat on top and bottom with larger border strips.

4. Lay stitched top on batting and pin together. Trim batting to match top. Baste and stitch in the stitching around the border.

5. On each backing piece, press ½" fold on one long side. Topstitch. Overlap topstitched edges, matching raw edges all around. Baste.

6. Place the ends of two binding strips perpendicular to each other, right sides together. Stitch diagonally as shown in Diagram A. Trim the seam allowances to ¼". Press open. Trim the beginning of binding at a 45° angle, matching the angle of the other seams. With wrong sides together, fold binding in half lengthwise. Press.

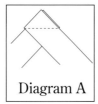

Diagram A

7. Starting in the middle of a side and leaving a 6" tail of binding loose, align the raw edges of the binding on the front edge. Begin sewing the binding to the pillow with ¼" seam allowance. Stop ¼" from the corner and backstitch to secure. Remove needle from border and trim threads.

8. Fold the binding up and back down, aligning the fold with the top edge of the pillow. Begin stitching ¼" from the binding fold, backstitch to secure. Continue sewing. Repeat for remaining three corners.

9. When the first side of the pillow is reached, leave at least 12" of border unbound and a 10"-12" binding tail. On a flat surface and with binding folded open, pin the ending tail along pillow edge. Smooth the beginning and ending tail over the ending tail. Following the cut edge of the beginning tail and using pencil, draw a line on the ending tail. Make certain that line is at a 45° angle to the binding long edges.

10. Fold the beginning tail out of the way and, to add the seam allowance, draw another line ½" out from the first line. *Note: The second line is a cutting line. Make certain it guides you to cut the binding tail ½" longer than the first line.* Cut the second line.

11. Place the ends right sides together. *Note: The points will be off-set a little so that the strips match ¼" in from the edge.* Join with ¼" seam allowance. Press seam allowance open. Press this section of binding in half. Finish sewing the binding to the pillow.

12. At each corner, fold the binding to back of pillow. Stitch the binding miters closed as shown in Diagram B.

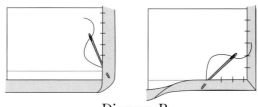

Diagram B

# YELLOW ROSE PILLOW

## STITCHING INFORMATION

Fabric: Aida 8, white

Stitch Count: 75w x 75h

Size: 8 count, 9⅜" square plus 2" beyond all around

Design size: 12" x 12"

## CUTTING INFORMATION

Borders: Cut two 4" x 13" pieces for sides. Cut two
4" x 9" pieces for top and bottom.

Batting: 19½" x 19½"

Backing: Cut two 19½" x 12½"

Binding: Cut three strips 2" x width of fabric

Trim design unit 2" beyond design

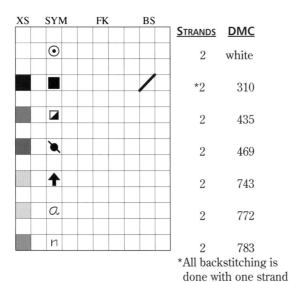

| XS | SYM | FK | BS | STRANDS | DMC |
|---|---|---|---|---|---|
| | ⊙ | | | 2 | white |
| ■ | ■ | | / | *2 | 310 |
| | ◪ | | | 2 | 435 |
| | ◣ | | | 2 | 469 |
| | ↑ | | | 2 | 743 |
| | a | | | 2 | 772 |
| | n | | | 2 | 783 |

*All backstitching is
done with one strand

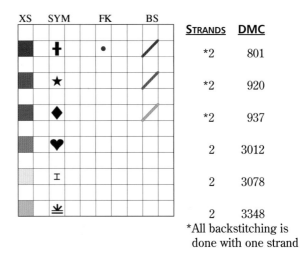

| XS | SYM | FK | BS | STRANDS | DMC |
|---|---|---|---|---|---|
| ■ | ✚ | • | / | *2 | 801 |
| ■ | ★ | | / | *2 | 920 |
| ■ | ◆ | | / | *2 | 937 |
| ■ | ♥ | | | 2 | 3012 |
| | ɪ | | | 2 | 3078 |
| ■ | ⚓ | | | 2 | 3348 |

*All backstitching is
done with one strand

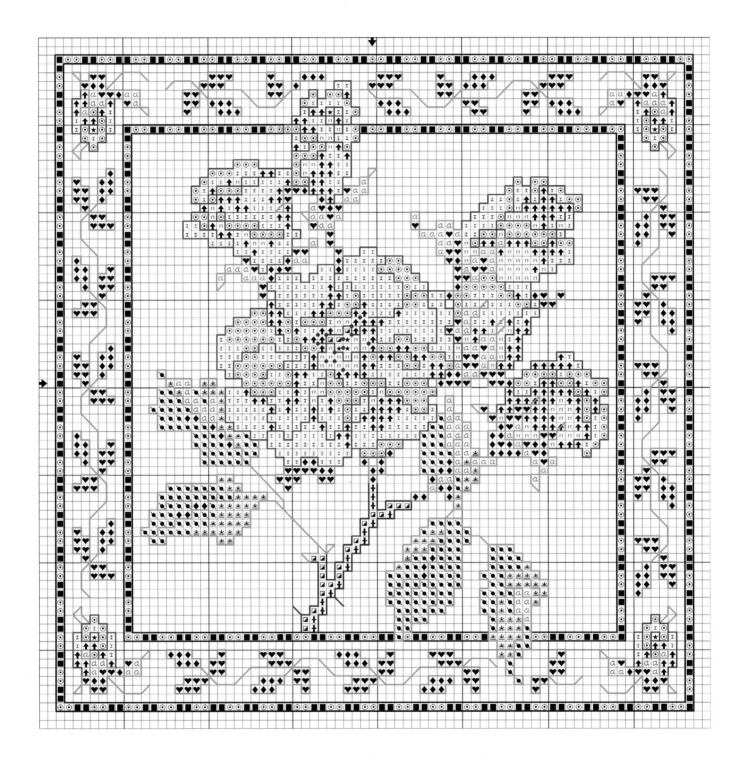

## STITCHING INFORMATION

Fabric: Aida 14, white

Stitch Count: 126w x 108h

Size: 14 count, 9" x 7⅝"

Design size: 8½" x 7½"

## CUTTING INFORMATION

Borders: Cut two 4" x width of fabric. Remove selvages from one strip and cut two 10" pieces. From remaining strip cut two 16¾" pieces.

Batting: Cut 15¾" x 18" piece

Backing: Cut two 15¾" x 11½"

Binding: Cut two 2" x width of fabric

Trim design unit 1¾" beyond design

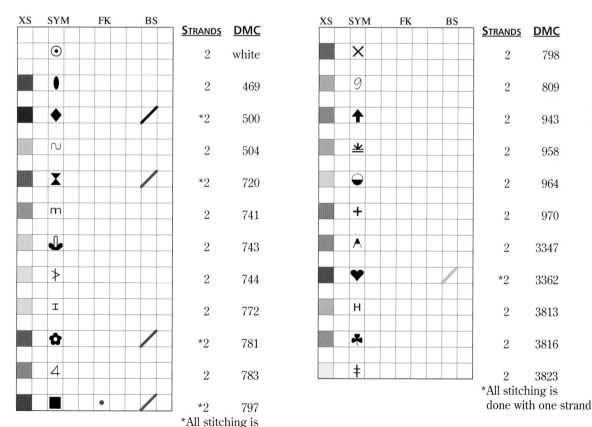

| XS | SYM | FK | BS | STRANDS | DMC |
|----|-----|----|----|---------|-----|
|  | ⊙ |  |  | 2 | white |
|  | ⬮ |  |  | 2 | 469 |
|  | ◆ |  | / | *2 | 500 |
|  | ∼ |  |  | 2 | 504 |
|  | ✕ |  | / | *2 | 720 |
|  | m |  |  | 2 | 741 |
|  | ⚓ |  |  | 2 | 743 |
|  | ⚲ |  |  | 2 | 744 |
|  | ɪ |  |  | 2 | 772 |
|  | ✿ |  | / | *2 | 781 |
|  | 4 |  |  | 2 | 783 |
|  | ■ | • | / | *2 | 797 |

*All stitching is done with one strand

| XS | SYM | FK | BS | STRANDS | DMC |
|----|-----|----|----|---------|-----|
|  | ✕ |  |  | 2 | 798 |
|  | 9 |  |  | 2 | 809 |
|  | ⬆ |  |  | 2 | 943 |
|  | ⚵ |  |  | 2 | 958 |
|  | ◓ |  |  | 2 | 964 |
|  | + |  |  | 2 | 970 |
|  | ⋀ |  |  | 2 | 3347 |
|  | ♥ |  | / | *2 | 3362 |
|  | H |  |  | 2 | 3813 |
|  | ♣ |  |  | 2 | 3816 |
|  | ‡ |  |  | 2 | 3823 |

*All stitching is done with one strand

Top Left

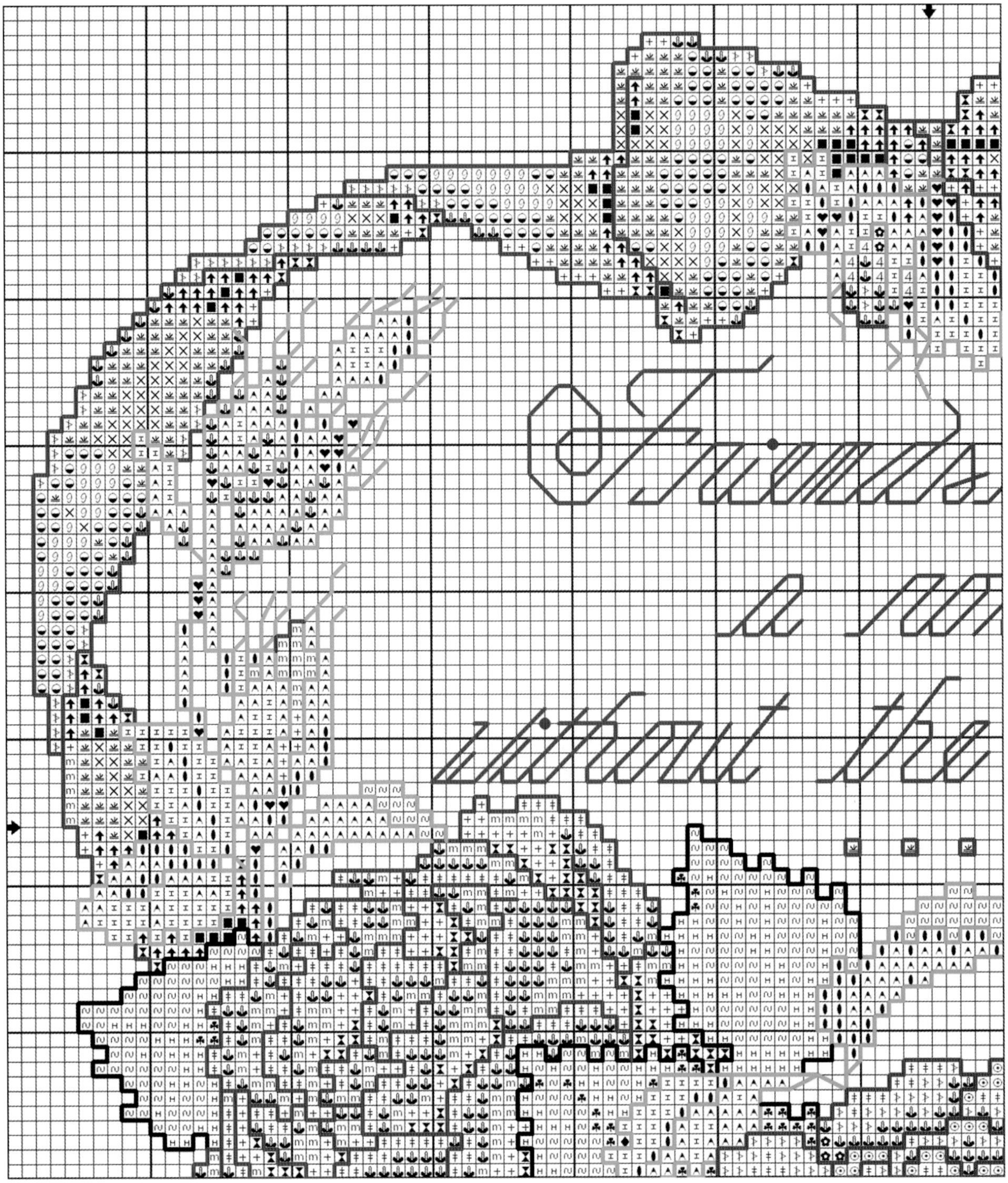

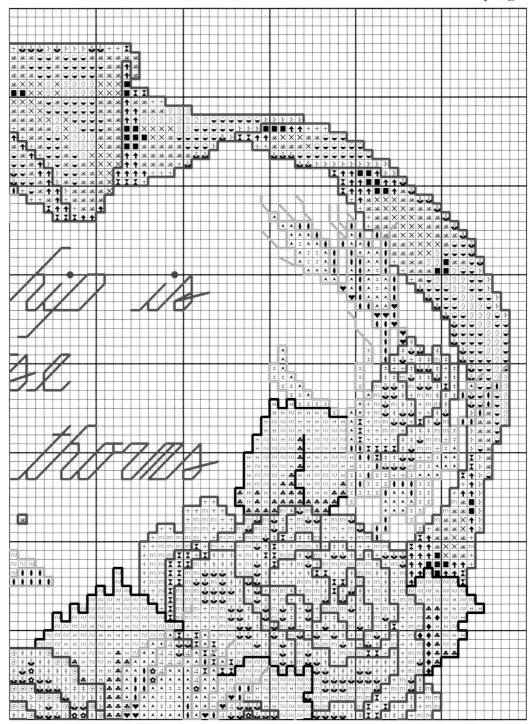

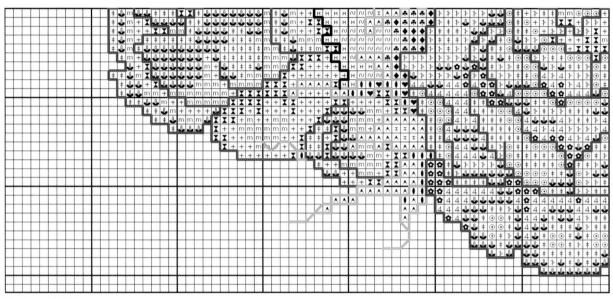

Bottom Left

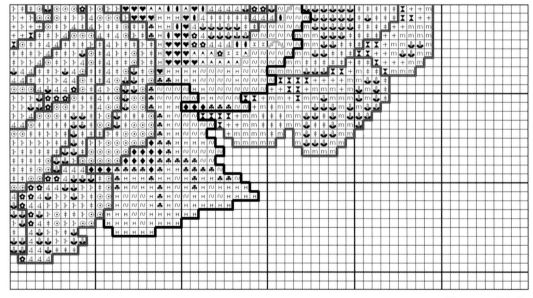

Bottom Right

## STITCHING INFORMATION

Fabric: Aida 14, white

Stitch Count: 140w x 98h

Size: 14 count, 10" x 7"

Design size: 9¼" x 7½"

## CUTTING INFORMATION

Borders: Cut two 4" x 10" pieces for sides.
Cut two 4" x 18" pieces for top and bottom.

Batting: 15¾" x 18"

Backing: Cut two 15¾" x 11½"

Binding: Cut 2" x 80" strip

Trim design unit 3" beyond design

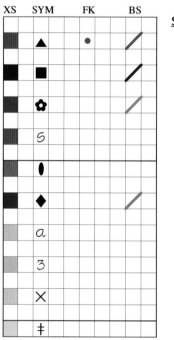
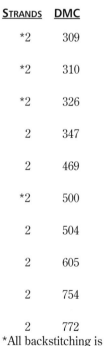

| XS | SYM | FK | BS | STRANDS | DMC |
|---|---|---|---|---|---|
| | ▲ | ● | / | *2 | 309 |
| | ■ | | / | *2 | 310 |
| | ✿ | | / | *2 | 326 |
| | S | | | 2 | 347 |
| | ❚ | | | 2 | 469 |
| | ◆ | | / | *2 | 500 |
| | a | | | 2 | 504 |
| | 3 | | | 2 | 605 |
| | ✕ | | | 2 | 754 |
| | ‡ | | | 2 | 772 |

*All backstitching is
done with one strand

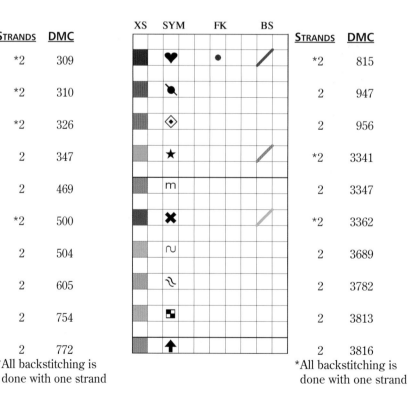

| XS | SYM | FK | BS | STRANDS | DMC |
|---|---|---|---|---|---|
| | ♥ | ● | / | *2 | 815 |
| | ❦ | | | 2 | 947 |
| | ◈ | | | 2 | 956 |
| | ★ | | / | *2 | 3341 |
| | m | | | 2 | 3347 |
| | ✖ | | / | *2 | 3362 |
| | ∿ | | | 2 | 3689 |
| | ⤳ | | | 2 | 3782 |
| | ▣ | | | 2 | 3813 |
| | ↑ | | | 2 | 3816 |

*All backstitching is
done with one strand

Top Left

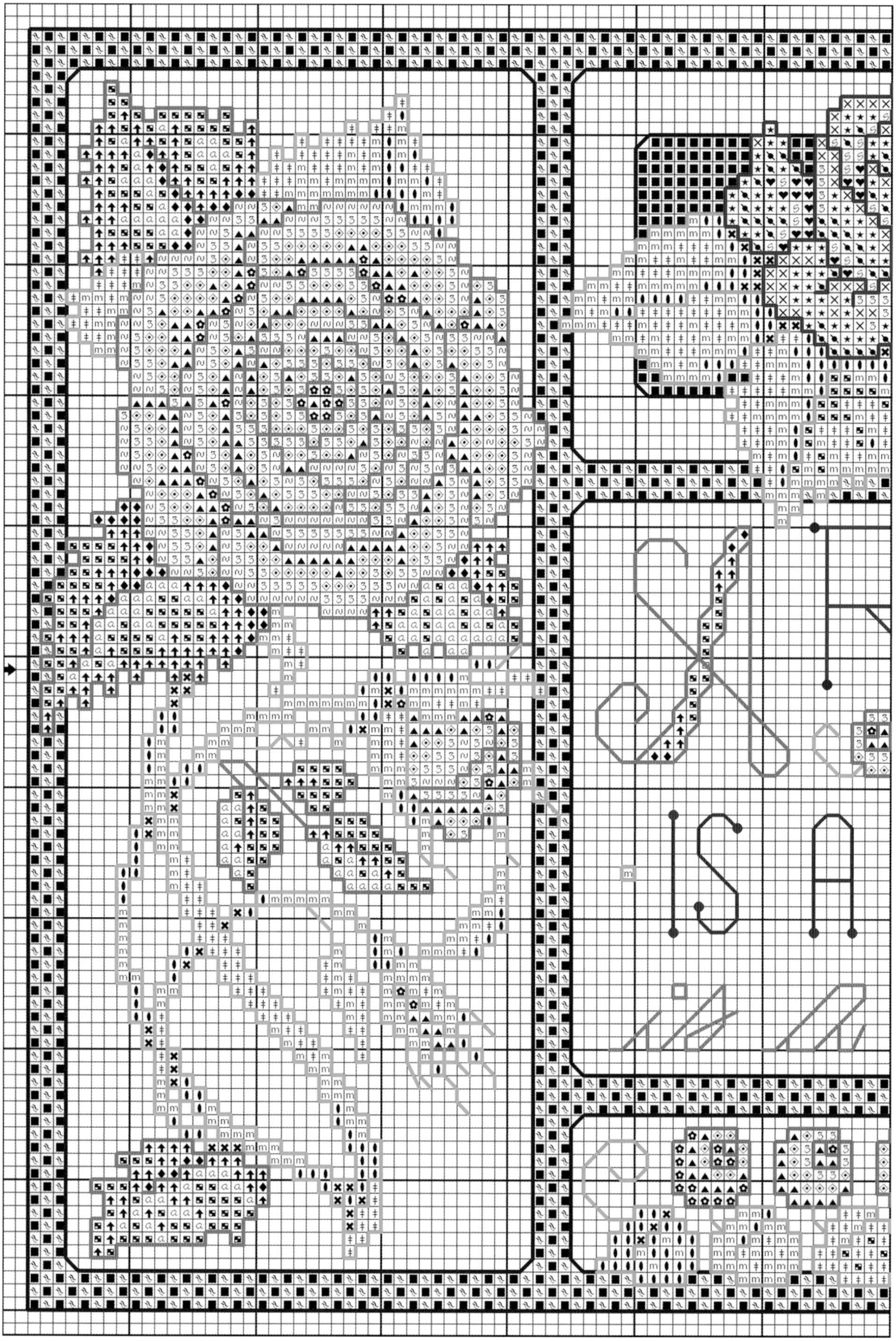

Top Right

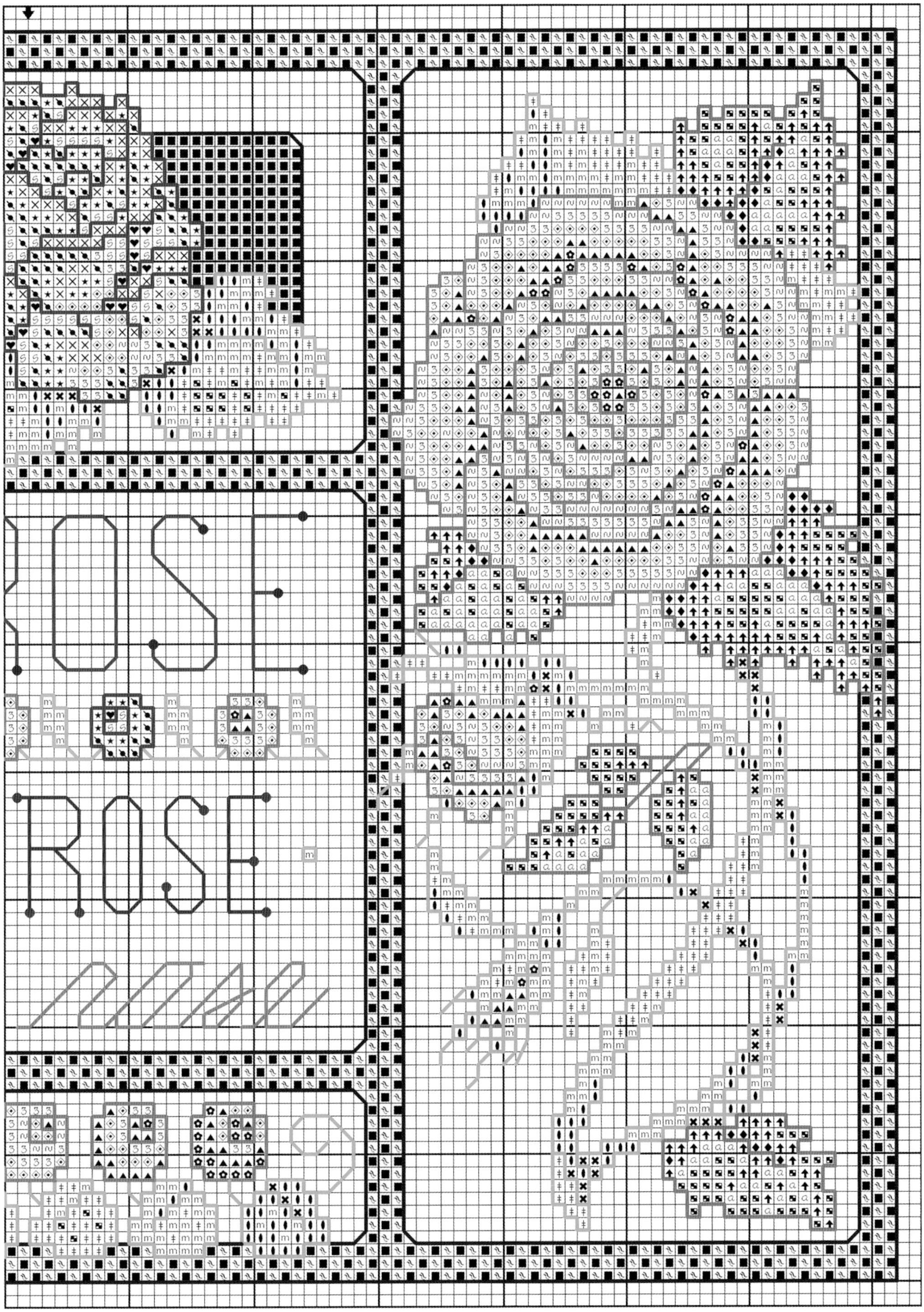

## STITCHING INFORMATION

Fabric: Aida 14, white

Stitch Count: 162w x 122h

Size: 14 count, 11½" x 8⅝"

Design size: 9½" x 7½"

## CUTTING INFORMATION

Borders: Cut two 4" x 10½" pieces for sides. Cut two 4" x 18½" pieces for top and bottom.

Batting: 16½" x 18½"

Backing: Cut two 16½" x 11½"

Binding: Cut 2" x 80" strip

Trim design unit 3" beyond design

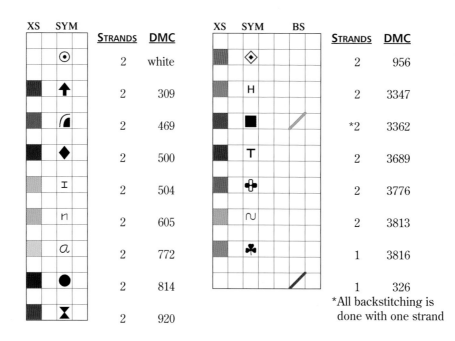

| XS | SYM | STRANDS | DMC |
|----|-----|---------|-----|
| | ⊙ | 2 | white |
| | ↑ | 2 | 309 |
| | ◖ | 2 | 469 |
| | ◆ | 2 | 500 |
| | I | 2 | 504 |
| | n | 2 | 605 |
| | a | 2 | 772 |
| | ● | 2 | 814 |
| | X | 2 | 920 |

| XS | SYM | BS | STRANDS | DMC |
|----|-----|----|---------|-----|
| | ◈ | | 2 | 956 |
| | H | | 2 | 3347 |
| | ■ | ╱ | *2 | 3362 |
| | T | | 2 | 3689 |
| | ✚ | | 2 | 3776 |
| | ∿ | | 2 | 3813 |
| | ♣ | | 1 | 3816 |
| | | ╱ | 1 | 326 |

*All backstitching is done with one strand

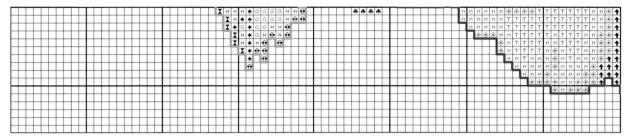

Bottom Left

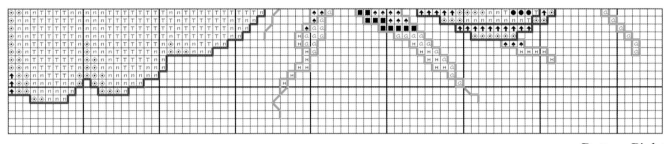

Bottom Right

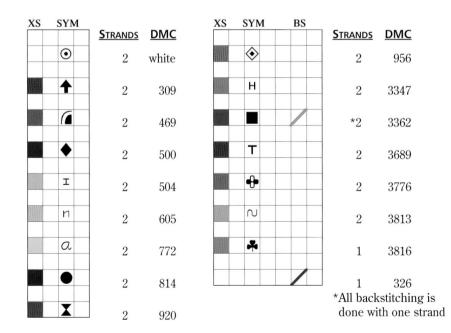

| XS | SYM | | STRANDS | DMC |
|---|---|---|---|---|
| | ⊙ | | 2 | white |
| | ↑ | | 2 | 309 |
| | ⌐ | | 2 | 469 |
| | ◆ | | 2 | 500 |
| | ɪ | | 2 | 504 |
| | n | | 2 | 605 |
| | α | | 2 | 772 |
| | ● | | 2 | 814 |
| | ✕ | | 2 | 920 |

| XS | SYM | BS | STRANDS | DMC |
|---|---|---|---|---|
| | ◈ | | 2 | 956 |
| | H | | 2 | 3347 |
| | ■ | ╱ | *2 | 3362 |
| | T | | 2 | 3689 |
| | ✚ | | 2 | 3776 |
| | ∼ | | 2 | 3813 |
| | ♣ | | 1 | 3816 |
| | | ╱ | 1 | 326 |

*All backstitching is
done with one strand

112

# MIXED BOUQUET

## STITCHING INFORMATION

Photograph on page 120

Fabric: Aida 14, white

Stitch Count: 197w x 196h

Size: 14 count, 14" x 14" plus ½" seam allowance on all sides

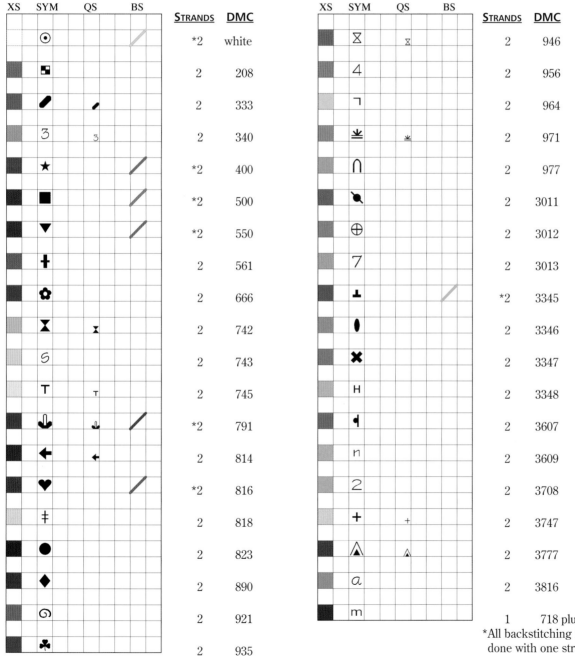

| XS | SYM | QS | BS | STRANDS | DMC |
|---|---|---|---|---|---|
| | ⊙ | | ╱ | *2 | white |
| | ◩ | | | 2 | 208 |
| | ▬ | ╱ | | 2 | 333 |
| | 3 | 3 | | 2 | 340 |
| | ★ | | ╱ | *2 | 400 |
| | ■ | | ╱ | *2 | 500 |
| | ▼ | | ╱ | *2 | 550 |
| | ✝ | | | 2 | 561 |
| | ✿ | | | 2 | 666 |
| | ✗ | ✗ | | 2 | 742 |
| | ꙅ | | | 2 | 743 |
| | T | T | | 2 | 745 |
| | ⚓ | ⚓ | ╱ | *2 | 791 |
| | ◄ | ◄ | | 2 | 814 |
| | ♥ | | ╱ | *2 | 816 |
| | ‡ | | | 2 | 818 |
| | ● | | | 2 | 823 |
| | ◆ | | | 2 | 890 |
| | ෆ | | | 2 | 921 |
| | ♣ | | | 2 | 935 |

*All backstitching is done with one strand

| XS | SYM | QS | BS | STRANDS | DMC |
|---|---|---|---|---|---|
| | ⊠ | ⊠ | | 2 | 946 |
| | 4 | | | 2 | 956 |
| | ⅂ | | | 2 | 964 |
| | ⚑ | ⚑ | | 2 | 971 |
| | ∩ | | | 2 | 977 |
| | ◕ | | | 2 | 3011 |
| | ⊕ | | | 2 | 3012 |
| | 7 | | | 2 | 3013 |
| | ⊥ | | ╱ | *2 | 3345 |
| | ◗ | | | 2 | 3346 |
| | ✖ | | | 2 | 3347 |
| | H | | | 2 | 3348 |
| | ◖ | | | 2 | 3607 |
| | n | | | 2 | 3609 |
| | 2 | | | 2 | 3708 |
| | ✛ | + | | 2 | 3747 |
| | ◬ | ◬ | | 2 | 3777 |
| | a | | | 2 | 3816 |
| | m | | | 1 | 718 plus 1 strand 915 |

*All backstitching is done with one strand

Top Left

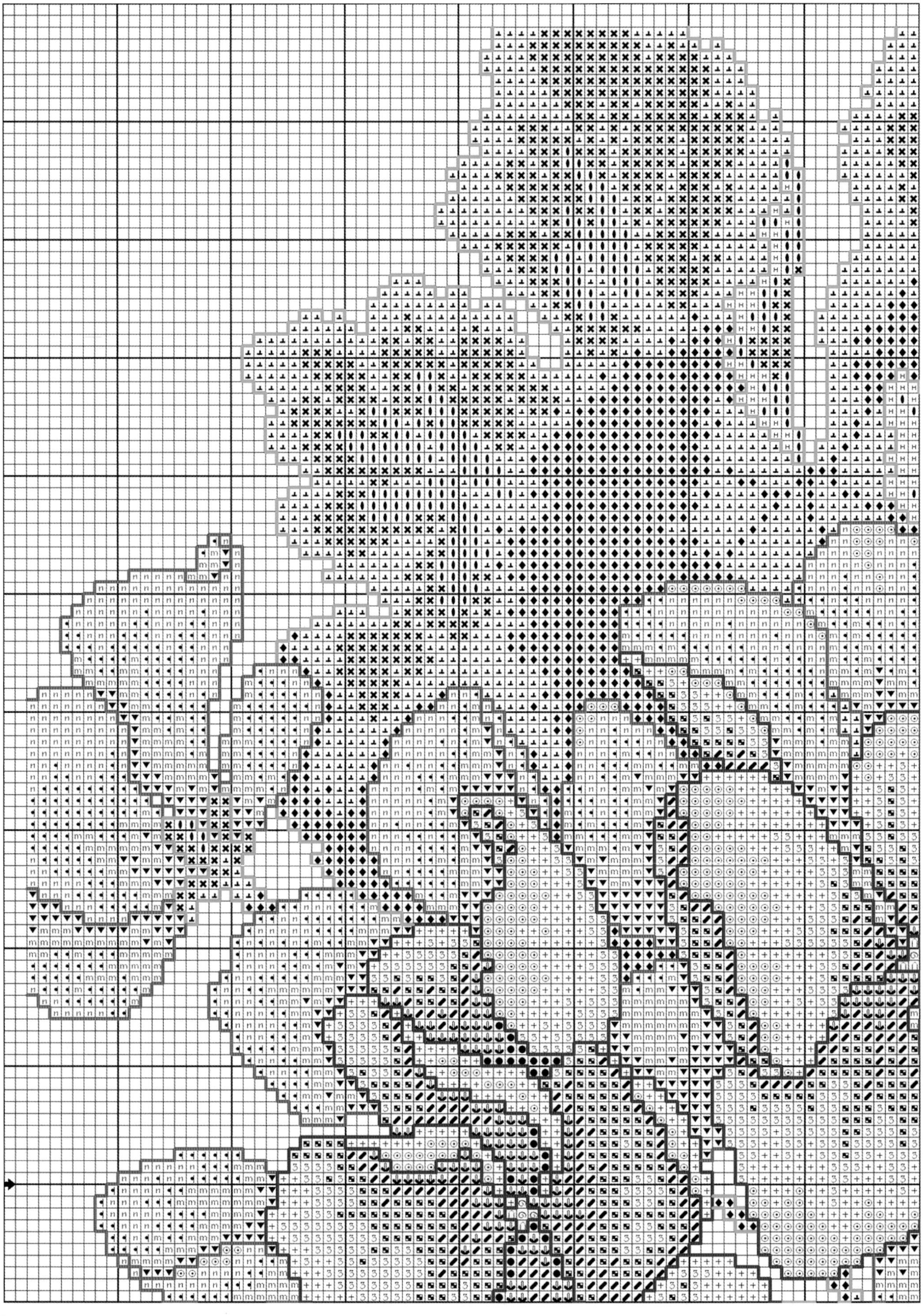

Top Center

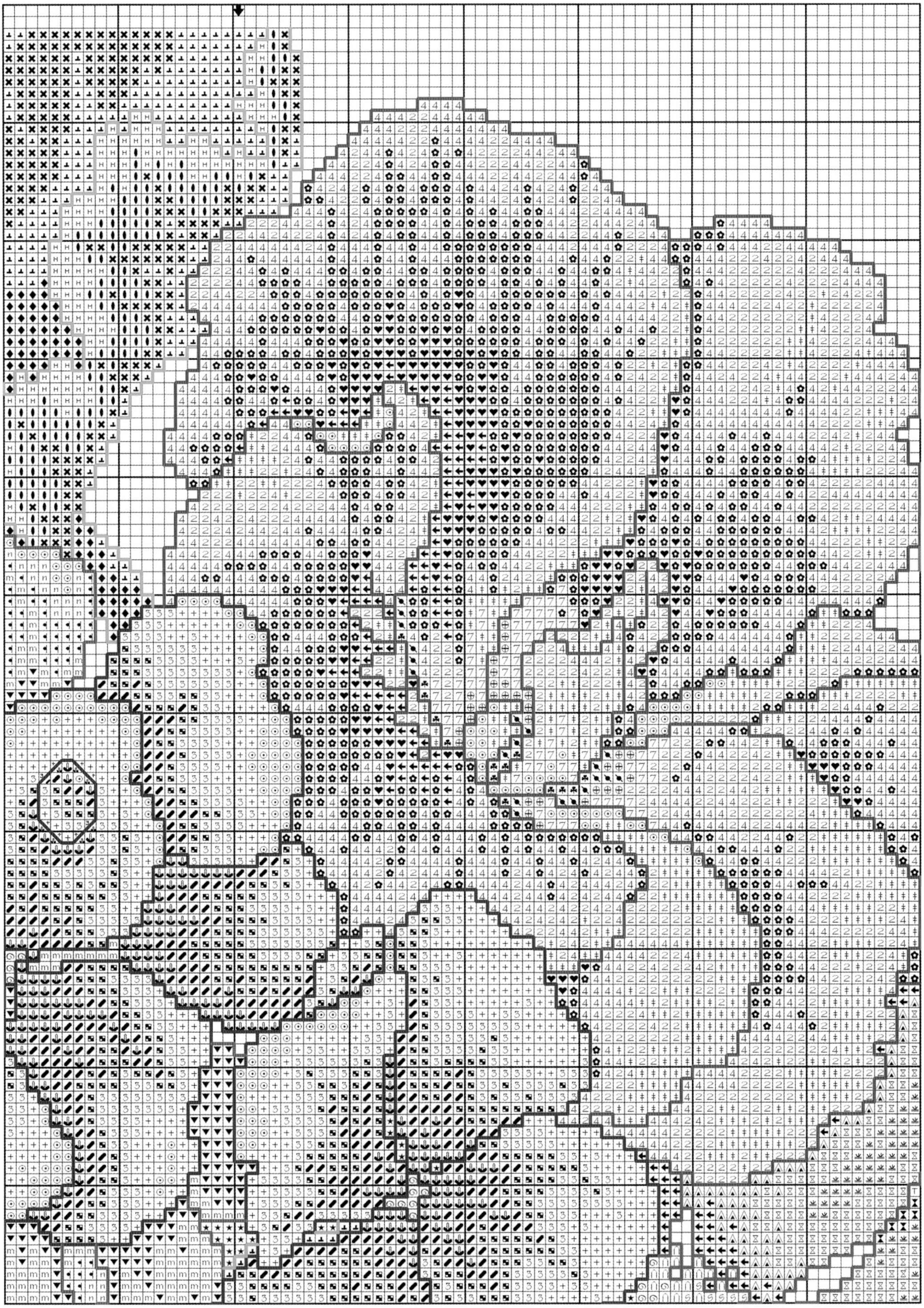

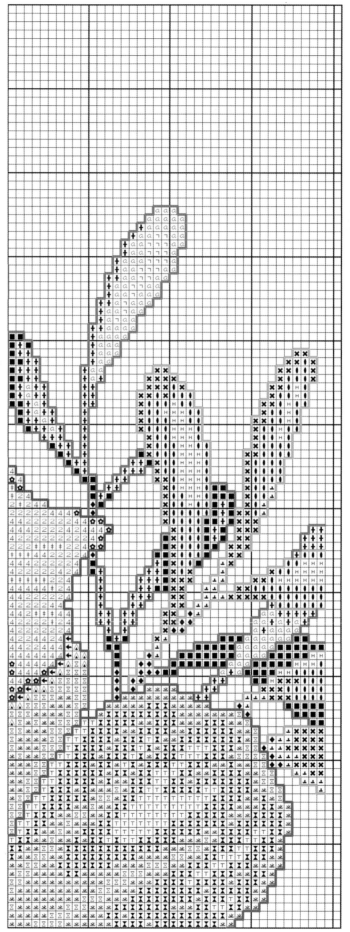

116

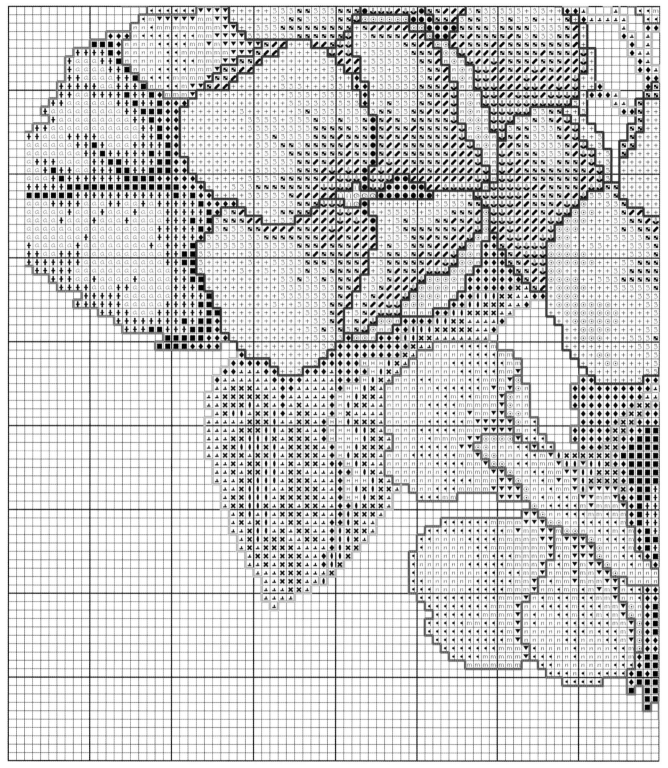

Bottom Left

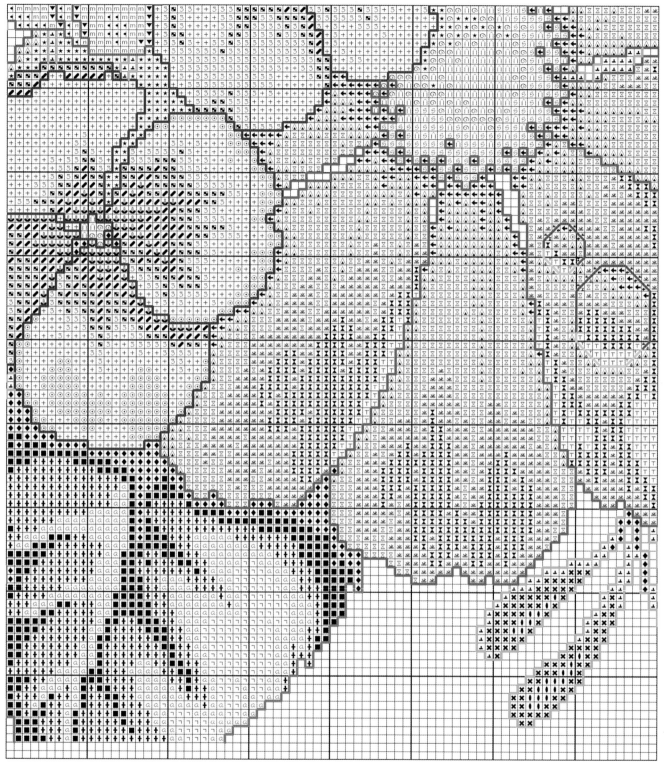

Bottom Center

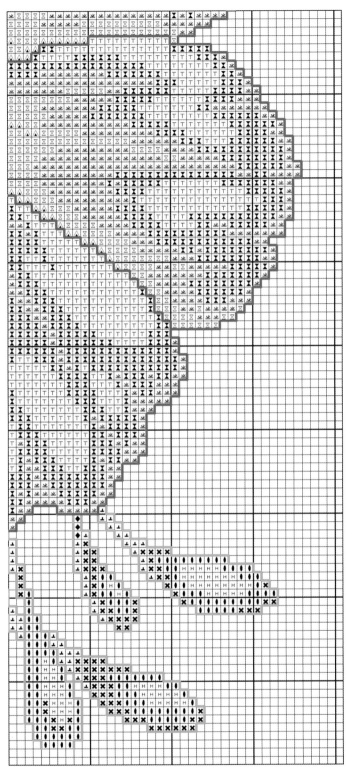

Bottom Right

## MATERIALS & SUPPLIES

- Aida 14, white
- Backing fabric
- Fabric (1 yd)
- Fabric hoop
- Fabric scissors
- Iron/ironing board
- Polyester fiberfill stuffing
- Sewing needle
- Sewing thread to match fabric
- Straight pins

## INSTRUCTIONS

1. With fabric in hoop, stitch desired design.

2. Remove finished cross-stitched piece from fabric hoop. Press, right side down.

3. Cut to size. Baste-stitch ½"-wide seam allowance on all sides. Refer to Baste Stitch on page 7. *Note: Be accurate. This basting line will be used later as guideline when backing is attached.*

4. Cut four strips of 7¼" x width of fabric. Trim strips to 40" long. With right sides together, sew short sides, forming circle. Press the seams open.

5. With wrong sides together, place raw edges together and press. Gather raw edge of ruffle, using ½" seam allowance to measure 58". Pin to cross-stitched piece, raw edges matching and ruffle evenly distributed. Baste-stitch along stitching line. Remove pins.

7. Cut two 15" x 8" pieces for backing. Place right sides together. On one long side, use ½" seam allowance to join pieces together, stitching 3" at each end and leaving a generous opening approximately 9" for turning and stuffing. Backstitch for extra strength. Refer to Backstitch on page 7. Press seam open.

8. With right sides together, sew cross-stitch piece to backing fabric along basting line (½" seam allowance). Turn right sides out and stuff. Slipstitch opening closed. Refer to Slipstitch on page 8.

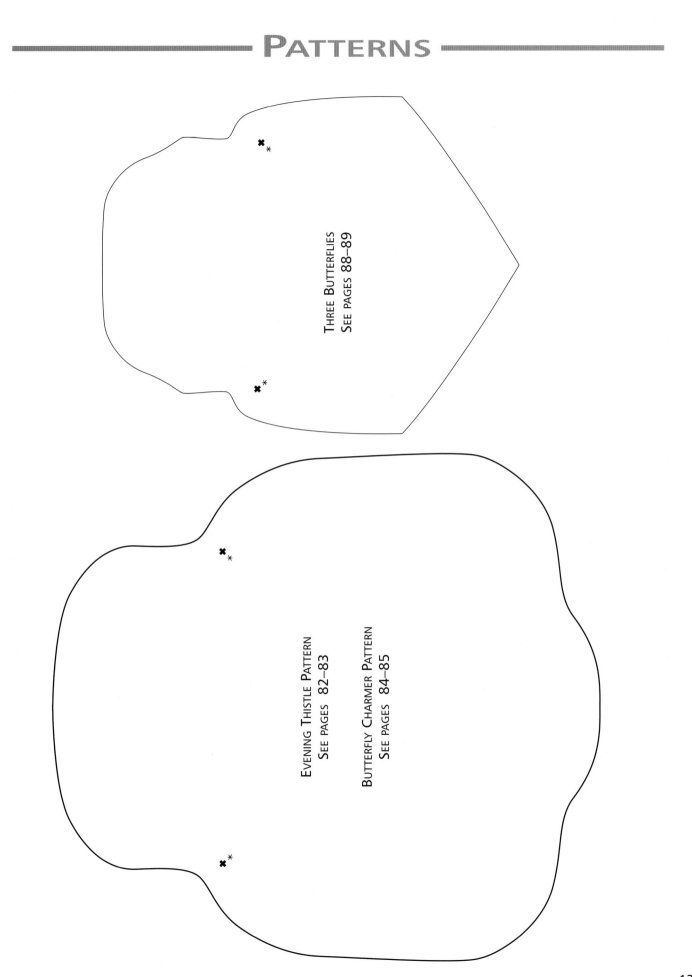

THREE BUTTERFLIES
SEE PAGES 88–89

EVENING THISTLE PATTERN
SEE PAGES 82–83

BUTTERFLY CHARMER PATTERN
SEE PAGES 84–85

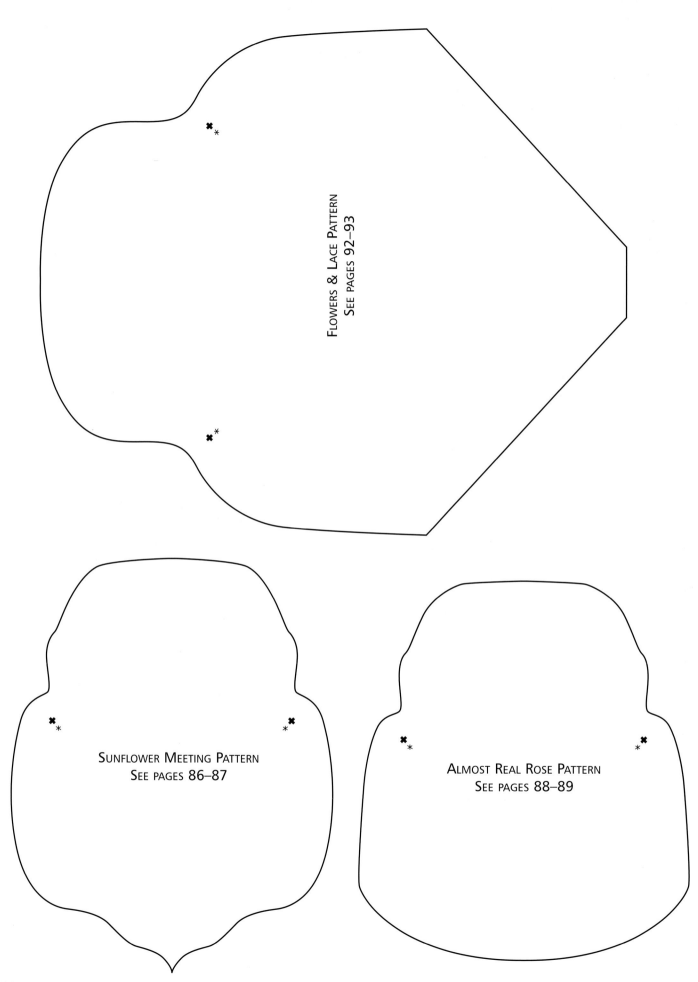

FLOWERS & LACE PATTERN
SEE PAGES 92–93

SUNFLOWER MEETING PATTERN
SEE PAGES 86–87

ALMOST REAL ROSE PATTERN
SEE PAGES 88–89

## ABOUT KOOLER DESIGN STUDIO, INC.

**CREATIVE DIRECTOR**
Donna Kooler

**EXECUTIVE VICE PRESIDENT**
Linda Gillum

**VICE PRESIDENT & BOOK EDITOR**
Priscilla Timm

**EDITOR-IN-CHIEF**
Judy Swager

**DESIGNERS**
Barbara Baatz Hillman, Linda Gillum,
Nancy Rossi, Jorja Hernandez, Sandy Orton,
Pam Johnson, Donna Yuen

**STAFF**
Marsha Hinkson, Maria Rodreguez,
Sara Angle, Jennifer Drake, Laurie Grant,
Virginia Hanley-Rivett, Char Randolph,
Joellen Angel, Helen Christensen,
Valarie MacDonald, Christine Mitchel

## ACKNOWLEDGMENTS

**DESIGNERS**
Linda Gillum 10–15, 29–33, 44–51

Jorja Heranadez 16–19, 41–43, 96–98

Barbara Baatz Hillman 20–27, 34–40, 52–79,
   82–93, 99–120

**EDITOR**
Karmen Quinney

**PHOTOGRAPHER**
Zac Williams

**PHOTOSTYLIST**
Annie Hampton

# ANCHOR CONVERSION CHART

| DMC | Anchor |
|-----|--------|
| B5200 | 1 |
| White | 2 |
| Ecru | 387 |
| 208 | 110 |
| 209 | 109 |
| 210 | 108 |
| 211 | 342 |
| 221 | 897 |
| 223 | 895 |
| 224 | 893 |
| 225 | 1026 |
| 300 | 352 |
| 301 | 1049 |
| 304 | 19 |
| 307 | 289 |
| 309 | 42 |
| 310 | 403 |
| 311 | 148 |
| 312 | 979 |
| 315 | 1019 |
| 316 | 1017 |
| 317 | 400 |
| 318 | 235 |
| 319 | 1044 |
| 320 | 215 |
| 321 | 47 |
| 322 | 978 |
| 326 | 59 |
| 327 | 101 |
| 333 | 119 |
| 334 | 977 |
| 335 | 40 |
| 336 | 150 |
| 340 | 118 |
| 341 | 117 |
| 347 | 1025 |
| 349 | 13 |
| 350 | 11 |
| 351 | 10 |
| 352 | 9 |
| 353 | 8 |
| 355 | 1014 |
| 356 | 1013 |
| 367 | 216 |

| DMC | Anchor |
|-----|--------|
| 368 | 214 |
| 369 | 1043 |
| 370 | 888 |
| 371 | 887 |
| 372 | 887 |
| 400 | 351 |
| 402 | 1047 |
| 407 | 914 |
| 413 | 236 |
| 414 | 235 |
| 415 | 398 |
| 420 | 374 |
| 422 | 372 |
| 433 | 358 |
| 434 | 310 |
| 435 | 365 |
| 436 | 363 |
| 437 | 362 |
| 444 | 291 |
| 445 | 288 |
| 451 | 233 |
| 452 | 232 |
| 453 | 231 |
| 469 | 267 |
| 470 | 266 |
| 471 | 265 |
| 472 | 253 |
| 498 | 1005 |
| 500 | 683 |
| 501 | 878 |
| 502 | 877 |
| 503 | 876 |
| 504 | 206 |
| 517 | 162 |
| 518 | 1039 |
| 519 | 1038 |
| 520 | 862 |
| 522 | 860 |
| 523 | 859 |
| 524 | 858 |
| 535 | 401 |
| 543 | 933 |
| 550 | 101 |
| 552 | 99 |
| 553 | 98 |

| DMC | Anchor |
|-----|--------|
| 554 | 95 |
| 561 | 212 |
| 562 | 210 |
| 563 | 208 |
| 564 | 206 |
| 580 | 924 |
| 581 | 281 |
| 597 | 1064 |
| 598 | 1062 |
| 600 | 59 |
| 601 | 63 |
| 602 | 57 |
| 603 | 62 |
| 604 | 55 |
| 605 | 1094 |
| 606 | 334 |
| 608 | 330 |
| 610 | 889 |
| 611 | 898 |
| 612 | 832 |
| 613 | 831 |
| 632 | 936 |
| 640 | 393 |
| 642 | 392 |
| 644 | 391 |
| 645 | 273 |
| 646 | 8581 |
| 647 | 1040 |
| 648 | 900 |
| 666 | 46 |
| 676 | 891 |
| 677 | 361 |
| 680 | 901 |
| 699 | 923 |
| 700 | 228 |
| 701 | 227 |
| 702 | 226 |
| 703 | 238 |
| 704 | 256 |
| 712 | 926 |
| 718 | 88 |
| 720 | 325 |
| 721 | 324 |
| 722 | 323 |
| 725 | 305 |

| DMC | Anchor |
|-----|--------|
| 726 | 295 |
| 727 | 293 |
| 729 | 890 |
| 730 | 845 |
| 731 | 281 |
| 732 | 281 |
| 733 | 280 |
| 734 | 279 |
| 738 | 361 |
| 739 | 366 |
| 740 | 316 |
| 741 | 304 |
| 742 | 303 |
| 743 | 302 |
| 744 | 301 |
| 745 | 300 |
| 746 | 275 |
| 747 | 158 |
| 754 | 1012 |
| 758 | 9575 |
| 760 | 1022 |
| 761 | 1021 |
| 762 | 234 |
| 772 | 259 |
| 775 | 128 |
| 776 | 24 |
| 778 | 968 |
| 780 | 309 |
| 781 | 308 |
| 782 | 308 |
| 783 | 307 |
| 791 | 178 |
| 792 | 941 |
| 793 | 176 |
| 794 | 175 |
| 796 | 133 |
| 797 | 132 |
| 798 | 146 |
| 799 | 145 |
| 800 | 144 |
| 801 | 359 |
| 806 | 169 |
| 807 | 168 |
| 809 | 130 |
| 813 | 161 |

| DMC | Anchor |
|-----|--------|
| 814 | 45 |
| 815 | 44 |
| 816 | 43 |
| 817 | 13 |
| 818 | 23 |
| 819 | 271 |
| 820 | 134 |
| 822 | 390 |
| 823 | 152 |
| 824 | 164 |
| 825 | 162 |
| 826 | 161 |
| 827 | 160 |
| 828 | 9159 |
| 829 | 906 |
| 830 | 277 |
| 831 | 277 |
| 832 | 907 |
| 833 | 874 |
| 834 | 874 |
| 838 | 1088 |
| 839 | 1086 |
| 840 | 1084 |
| 841 | 1082 |
| 842 | 1080 |
| 844 | 1041 |
| 869 | 375 |
| 890 | 218 |
| 891 | 35 |
| 892 | 33 |
| 893 | 27 |
| 894 | 26 |
| 895 | 1044 |
| 898 | 380 |
| 899 | 38 |
| 900 | 333 |
| 902 | 897 |
| 904 | 258 |
| 905 | 257 |
| 906 | 256 |
| 907 | 255 |
| 909 | 923 |
| 910 | 230 |
| 911 | 205 |
| 912 | 209 |

| | | | | | | | | | |
|---|---|---|---|---|---|---|---|---|---|
| 913 | 204 | 977 | 1002 | 3371 | 382 | 3790 | 904 | | |
| 915 | 1029 | 986 | 246 | 3607 | 87 | 3799 | 236 | | |
| 917 | 89 | 987 | 244 | 3608 | 86 | 3801 | 1098 | | |
| 918 | 341 | 988 | 243 | 3609 | 85 | 3802 | 1019 | | |
| 919 | 340 | 989 | 242 | 3685 | 1028 | 3803 | 69 | | |
| 920 | 1004 | 991 | 1076 | 3687 | 68 | 3804 | 63 | | |
| 921 | 1003 | 992 | 1072 | 3688 | 75 | 3805 | 62 | | |
| 922 | 1003 | 993 | 1070 | 3689 | 49 | 3806 | 62 | | |
| 924 | 851 | 995 | 410 | 3705 | 35 | 3807 | 122 | | |
| 926 | 850 | 996 | 433 | 3706 | 33 | 3808 | 1068 | | |
| 927 | 849 | 3011 | 856 | 3708 | 31 | 3809 | 1066 | | |
| 928 | 274 | 3012 | 855 | 3712 | 1023 | 3810 | 1066 | | |
| 930 | 1035 | 3013 | 853 | 3713 | 1020 | 3811 | 1060 | | |
| 931 | 1034 | 3021 | 905 | 3716 | 25 | 3812 | 188 | | |
| 932 | 1033 | 3022 | 8581 | 3721 | 896 | 3813 | 875 | | |
| 934 | 862 | 3023 | 899 | 3722 | 1027 | 3814 | 1074 | | |
| 935 | 861 | 3024 | 388 | 3726 | 1018 | 3815 | 877 | | |
| 936 | 846 | 3031 | 905 | 3727 | 1016 | 3816 | 876 | | |
| 937 | 268 | 3032 | 898 | 3731 | 76 | 3817 | 875 | | |
| 938 | 381 | 3033 | 387 | 3733 | 75 | 3818 | 923 | | |
| 939 | 152 | 3041 | 871 | 3740 | 872 | 3819 | 278 | | |
| 943 | 189 | 3042 | 870 | 3743 | 869 | 3820 | 306 | | |
| 945 | 881 | 3045 | 888 | 3746 | 1030 | 3821 | 305 | | |
| 946 | 332 | 3046 | 887 | 3747 | 120 | 3822 | 295 | | |
| 947 | 330 | 3047 | 852 | 3750 | 1036 | 3823 | 386 | | |
| 948 | 1011 | 3051 | 845 | 3752 | 1032 | 3824 | 8 | | |
| 950 | 4146 | 3052 | 844 | 3753 | 1031 | 3825 | 323 | | |
| 951 | 1010 | 3053 | 843 | 3755 | 140 | 3826 | 1049 | | |
| 954 | 203 | 3064 | 883 | 3756 | 1037 | 3827 | 311 | | |
| 955 | 203 | 3072 | 397 | 3760 | 162 | 3828 | 373 | | |
| 956 | 40 | 3078 | 292 | 3761 | 928 | 3829 | 901 | | |
| 957 | 50 | 3325 | 129 | 3765 | 170 | 3830 | 5975 | | |
| 958 | 187 | 3326 | 36 | 3766 | 167 | | | | |
| 959 | 186 | 3328 | 1024 | 3768 | 779 | | | | |
| 961 | 76 | 3340 | 329 | 3770 | 1009 | | | | |
| 962 | 75 | 3341 | 328 | 3772 | 1007 | | | | |
| 963 | 23 | 3345 | 268 | 3773 | 1008 | | | | |
| 964 | 185 | 3346 | 267 | 3774 | 778 | | | | |
| 966 | 240 | 3347 | 266 | 3776 | 1048 | | | | |
| 970 | 925 | 3348 | 264 | 3777 | 1015 | | | | |
| 971 | 316 | 3350 | 77 | 3778 | 1013 | | | | |
| 972 | 298 | 3354 | 74 | 3779 | 868 | | | | |
| 973 | 290 | 3362 | 263 | 3781 | 1050 | | | | |
| 975 | 357 | 3363 | 262 | 3782 | 388 | | | | |
| 976 | 1001 | 3364 | 261 | 3787 | 904 | | | | |

**VARIEGATED COLORS**

| | |
|---|---|
| 48 | 1207 |
| 51 | 1220 |
| 52 | 1209 |
| 53 | —— |
| 57 | 1203 |
| 61 | 1218 |
| 62 | 1201 |
| 67 | 1212 |
| 69 | 1218 |
| 75 | 1206 |
| 90 | 1217 |
| 91 | 1211 |
| 92 | 1215 |
| 93 | 1210 |
| 94 | 1216 |
| 95 | 1209 |
| 99 | 1204 |
| 101 | 1213 |
| 102 | 1209 |
| 103 | 1210 |
| 104 | 1217 |
| 105 | 1218 |
| 106 | 1203 |
| 107 | 1203 |
| 108 | 1220 |
| 111 | 1218 |
| 112 | 1201 |
| 113 | 1210 |
| 114 | 1213 |
| 115 | 1206 |
| 121 | 1210 |
| 122 | 1215 |
| 123 | —— |
| 124 | 1210 |
| 125 | 1213 |
| 126 | 1209 |

# METRIC CONVERSION CHARTS

mm-millimeters  cm-centimeters
inches to millimeters and centimeters

| inches | mm | cm | inches | cm | inches | cm |
|--------|-----|------|--------|------|--------|-------|
| ⅛ | 3 | 0.3 | 9 | 22.9 | 30 | 76.2 |
| ¼ | 6 | 0.6 | 10 | 25.4 | 31 | 78.7 |
| ⅜ | 10 | 1.0 | 11 | 27.9 | 32 | 81.3 |
| ½ | 13 | 1.3 | 12 | 30.5 | 33 | 83.8 |
| ⅝ | 16 | 1.6 | 13 | 33.0 | 34 | 86.4 |
| ¾ | 19 | 1.9 | 14 | 35.6 | 35 | 88.9 |
| ⅞ | 22 | 2.2 | 15 | 38.1 | 36 | 91.4 |
| 1 | 25 | 2.5 | 16 | 40.6 | 37 | 94.0 |
| 1¼ | 32 | 3.2 | 17 | 43.2 | 38 | 96.5 |
| 1½ | 38 | 3.8 | 18 | 45.7 | 39 | 99.1 |
| 1¾ | 44 | 4.4 | 19 | 48.3 | 40 | 101.6 |
| 2 | 51 | 5.1 | 20 | 50.8 | 41 | 104.1 |
| 2½ | 64 | 6.4 | 21 | 53.3 | 42 | 106.7 |
| 3 | 76 | 7.6 | 22 | 55.9 | 43 | 109.2 |
| 3½ | 89 | 8.9 | 23 | 58.4 | 44 | 111.8 |
| 4 | 102 | 10.2 | 24 | 61.0 | 45 | 114.3 |
| 4½ | 114 | 11.4 | 25 | 63.5 | 46 | 116.8 |
| 5 | 127 | 12.7 | 26 | 66.0 | 47 | 119.4 |
| 6 | 152 | 15.2 | 27 | 68.6 | 48 | 121.9 |
| 7 | 178 | 17.8 | 28 | 71.1 | 49 | 124.5 |
| 8 | 203 | 20.3 | 29 | 73.7 | 50 | 127.0 |

## yards to meters

| yards | meters | yards | meters | yards | meters | yards | meters | yards | meters |
|-------|--------|-------|--------|-------|--------|-------|--------|-------|--------|
| ⅛ | 0.11 | 2⅛ | 1.94 | 4⅛ | 3.77 | 6⅛ | 5.60 | 8⅛ | 7.43 |
| ¼ | 0.23 | 2¼ | 2.06 | 4¼ | 3.89 | 6¼ | 5.72 | 8¼ | 7.54 |
| ⅜ | 0.34 | 2⅜ | 2.17 | 4⅜ | 4.00 | 6⅜ | 5.83 | 8⅜ | 7.66 |
| ½ | 0.46 | 2½ | 2.29 | 4½ | 4.11 | 6½ | 5.94 | 8½ | 7.77 |
| ⅝ | 0.57 | 2⅝ | 2.40 | 4⅝ | 4.23 | 6⅝ | 6.06 | 8⅝ | 7.89 |
| ¾ | 0.69 | 2¾ | 2.51 | 4¾ | 4.34 | 6¾ | 6.17 | 8¾ | 8.00 |
| ⅞ | 0.80 | 2⅞ | 2.63 | 4⅞ | 4.46 | 6⅞ | 6.29 | 8⅞ | 8.12 |
| 1 | 0.91 | 3 | 2.74 | 5 | 4.57 | 7 | 6.40 | 9 | 8.23 |
| 1⅛ | 1.03 | 3⅛ | 2.86 | 5⅛ | 4.69 | 7⅛ | 6.52 | 9⅛ | 8.34 |
| 1¼ | 1.14 | 3¼ | 2.97 | 5¼ | 4.80 | 7¼ | 6.63 | 9¼ | 8.46 |
| 1⅜ | 1.26 | 3⅜ | 3.09 | 5⅜ | 4.91 | 7⅜ | 6.74 | 9⅜ | 8.57 |
| 1½ | 1.37 | 3½ | 3.20 | 5½ | 5.03 | 7½ | 6.86 | 9½ | 8.69 |
| 1⅝ | 1.49 | 3⅝ | 3.31 | 5⅝ | 5.14 | 7⅝ | 6.97 | 9⅝ | 8.80 |
| 1¾ | 1.60 | 3¾ | 3.43 | 5¾ | 5.26 | 7¾ | 7.09 | 9¾ | 8.92 |
| 1⅞ | 1.71 | 3⅞ | 3.54 | 5⅞ | 5.37 | 7⅞ | 7.20 | 9⅞ | 9.03 |
| 2 | 1.83 | 4 | 3.66 | 6 | 5.49 | 8 | 7.32 | 10 | 9.14 |

# INDEX